Contents

C000127569

Key Stage One

Step by Step Art Books are available from all good Educational Bookshops and by mail order from:

Topical Resources, P.O. Box 329, Broughton, Preston, Lancashire. PR3 5LT

Topical Resources publishes a range of Educational Materials for use in Primary Schools and Pre-School Nurseries and Playgroups.

For the latest catalogue
Tel 01772 863158 / Fax 01772 866153
e.mail: sales@topical-resources.co.uk
Visit our Website at: www.topical-resources.co.uk

Copyright © 2005 Dianne Williams

Printed in Great Britain for 'Topical Resources', Publishers of Educational Materials, P.O. Box 329, Broughton, Preston, Lancashire PR3 5LT by T.Snape & Company Limited, Boltons Court, Preston, Lancashire.

Designed by Paul Sealey Illustration & Design, 3 Wentworth Drive, Thornton, Lancashire.

First Published September 2005.

ISBN 1 872977 92 8

Key Stage

Introduction

Artists, craftworkers and designers have always used the world around them in its varied form as a stimulus for their work. The weather, the seasons, buildings, landscapes, seascapes etc. have all provided inspiration and ideas for a wide range of art work using different materials and techniques. This book aims to help the non- specialist art teacher to use the same types of stimulus for Art and Design work whilst linking it with the approaches to Geography in the National Curriculum for both Key Stage One and Key Stage Two.

The practical activities are designed to introduce and encourage children to develop skills and explore a range of different techniques using both two and three dimensional materials. These include drawing, painting, printing, collage, textiles and 3D as well as ICT where appropriate.

The book is divided into topics and there are several separate activities for each topic. Each activity has a 'talk about' section, a list of the materials needed, instructions on how to undertake the work plus suggestions as to how the finished work could be displayed. The activities, the skills involved and the materials used, cover much of the content of the National Curriculum for Art and Design outlined for both Key Stage One and Key Stage Two.

Each activity is illustrated for guidance and all have been tried and tested in the classroom. I am most grateful to the schools and the children who have provided such stunning work to illustrate this book. I feel it readily shows the creative links possible between these two subject areas and how they can easily be linked to enrich and re-enforce learning in both Geography and Art and Design. I hope the activities when undertaken in your school will have a similar result.

Dianne Williams

Schools which have provided work for this book include:
*   Christ Church C.E. Primary, Lancaster
*   Deepdale Infants School, Preston
*   Haslingden County Primary School
*   Kirkham St Michael's C.E. Primary
*   Manor Beach Primary School
*   Moss Side Primary School, Leyland
*   Northern Primary School, Bacup
*   St Gregory's Catholic Primary, Chorley
*   St Teresa's Catholic Primary, UpHolland
*   Tarleton Holy Trinity C.E.School
*   Weeton County Primary School
*   Whalley C.E. Primary School
with special thanks to my new friend Katy Downs.

Many other Lancashire schools have also offered inspiration for this work.

Around Our School - the local area

The School Building

Equipment Needed

Drawing pencils, pieces of white paper A4 size for initial sketches, larger pieces of grey sugar paper A3 size for paintings, white chalk, oil pastel crayons, paint, brushes and small pieces of card to use as mixing palettes. Pieces of coloured paper, scissors and glue if the initial sketches are going to be developed as collages and white A3 paper. Photographs of the school building from different view points.

Talk About

- The shape of the building as seen from the playground. The different individual parts of the building e.g. the roof, walls, windows and doors etc. and how they fit together. Which are the biggest parts and which are the smallest?
- The colours and textures seen on the building and the different materials used in its making.
- Working outside and making sketches of the building or making sketches inside from photographs - after first identifying where the photographs have been taken from. Using the photographs to add details to their sketches.
- Developing the sketches on A3 paper and adding colour to these using either paint or collage materials. The colours seen on the building that will need mixing or finding in paint and collage material.
- Cutting coloured paper into small pieces to use for collage. Drawing in details with oil pastel crayons.

Doing

- Using pencils and A4 paper, make a sketch of the school building. You will need to do plenty of looking and re- looking as you work to collect all the information and details you need.
- Draw a second, larger sketch of the school on A3 paper using chalk if the paper is grey, and pencil if it is white. Outline the large shapes first before adding the smaller ones.
- Mixing the colours of paint needed and filling in the large areas, drawing in details like tiles and bricks etc. using oil pastel crayons when the paint is dry. Outline windows, doors etc. In the same way or collect the colours needed in collage material, cutting, arranging and sticking pieces to fill the large shapes before using oil pastel crayon to draw in details.

Display

Mount and arrange the paintings and collages around the edge of the block of photographs of the school from which the children have worked.

Alternatively one of the original sketches could be traced by a child on an overhead projector sheet, and beamed up on to paper on a the wall to make a large image. This large image then traced on the paper could be worked on collaboratively by the whole class. Written work could be added below.

From Home to School

Equipment Needed

Wax crayons, oil pastel crayons, pieces of grey sugar paper A3 size, paint, brushes and pieces of card to use as mixing palettes. Pictures of the different types of houses in the local environment. A map of the area surrounding school with the street names on it. A computer and a printer.

Talk About

- The name of the street where they live and where it is on the map.
- How they come to school and what they pass or see on their way to school.
- The sort of house they live in. The houses in the pictures and where they are in the locality. Who lives in the same street as them.
- Making a piece of work that shows both houses and people.
- The colours needed for the houses and the colours needed for the people.
- Which colours can be found and which colours need to be made.
- How to mix those colours.
- Painting first and then adding extra details by drawing on the work with wax crayon or oil pastels once the paint is dry.

Albert Road

East Park Street

Oak Tree Avenue

- Draw with your finger on the paper first the size of the the houses and where they are going to be on the paper, and then the size of the people and where they are going to go. This way you can easily change your mind if they are too big or too small!
- Mix a pale shade of paint e.g. grey, and with a paint brush, draw in the main shapes (outlines) of the houses and people. Make sure one of them is you!
- Now mix the other colours you need and fill in these shapes.
- When the paint is dry use the crayons to draw in extra details e.g. window frames, expressions on the faces etc.
- Use the computer to write the name of your road or street in large letters and print it out.

Doing

- Get a piece of A3 paper and decide which way up it needs to be for your work - if you are going to paint a row of houses, landscape would be best, if it is only a couple of houses then portrait way would be better.
- Decide how many people you are going to put in your picture - just you and your mum or dad or lots of people on their way to school. Draw yourself outside your house even if you later get in a car to travel to school.

Display

Mount the pieces of work individually and display them in rows with identical sized spaces between them. Mount the street names on separate pieces of paper and display them under the appropriate painting. Display a map of the area on a flat surface under and adjacent to the work. Mark on this map the same street names the children have identified in their work.

A Sense of Place

Equipment Needed

Pieces of white paper A4 size, pieces of coloured paper A4 size, scissors, glue, drawing pencils and a collection of boxes of different sizes.

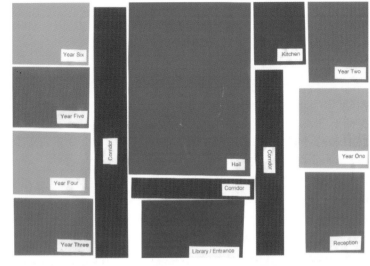

Talk About

- The different types of rooms in the school and what they are called.
- Which are the biggest, which are the smallest and which are the same size?
- The rooms they go into and use in school and those they don't use.
- Which rooms are next to one another.
- Sorting the boxes into sizes to match the rooms described i.e. those that are the same size, those that are big and those that are small.
- Arranging the boxes on the floor or on a table top next to each other as though they were rooms in school.
- Putting the names of the rooms in each of the boxes e.g. year one, library etc.
- Describing the shape of the finished building, the shape and size of the rooms and where the room they are now in is in the plan.
- Describing the route from e.g. their room to the hall etc.
- Drawing in pencil, a plan of the school after carefully looking at the arrangement and shapes of the boxes.
- Cutting coloured paper into smaller pieces to fill the shapes that have been drawn.

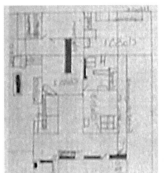

Doing

- Select in a group the boxes to make the plan of the school and arrange them in the way you feel they should fit together, side by side, to match the shape of the school.
- Discuss the arrangement, the positions and sizes of the different boxes and what they represent.

- Individually get a piece of A4 paper and a pencil, look carefully at the arrangement of the boxes then draw their shapes and how they fit together.
- Choose pieces of coloured paper and cut them into smaller shapes to fill each of the outlines that have been drawn - use a different colour for each shape. Glue the cut coloured paper inside the drawn outlines to complete a collage of the shape / plan of the school.

Display

If there are any original plans of the school building use these as a centre piece in the middle of the display with the collages individually mounted around the edge. If not then arrange the mounted collages as a grid with equal spaces between them. Arrange the box plan of the school (with each room labelled) on a surface adjacent to or under the display.

What's Outside?

Equipment Needed
Grey sugar paper A4 size and wax crayons in assorted colours.

Talk About
- The view from the classroom window - what can be seen close to the window and what can be seen in the distance.
- The view from other windows in the school - what is the same or similar to the view from their classroom and what is different.
- Objects e.g. trees or buildings that are in front of things in the view and those that are behind.
- What is big in the view they can see and what is small.
- Looking carefully at the view before starting to draw and also whilst drawing.
- Drawing only what can be seen through the window using the window frame as the outline to the view.
- Drawing outline shapes first with a pale colour of wax crayon before filling in and adding detail. Pressing firmly with wax crayon to get a rich covering of colour when completing the drawing.
- Using the shape of the paper to match the shape of the window i.e. either landscape or portrait style.

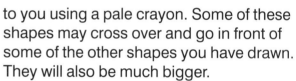

Doing
- Get a piece of grey sugar paper and some wax crayons.
- Look carefully at the view from the classroom window before choosing a pale crayon and lightly draw the shapes you can see in the distance - these will need to be small.
- Now draw, again with a pale crayon, the shapes that you can see in front of the small shapes. They will need to be slightly bigger.
- Finally, draw the shapes you can see nearest to you using a pale crayon. Some of these shapes may cross over and go in front of some of the other shapes you have drawn. They will also be much bigger.
- Find the colours of the crayons you need for the small shapes in the distance and colour these in. Now find the colours for the shapes in the middle of the picture and colour these in. Finally find the colours for the shapes in the front of your picture and fill them in. Press down firmly with the crayons for a rich covering of colour. Last of all, use the crayons to over draw and add in any details e.g. window frames, plant pots etc.

Display
Mount the work individually and display it around a block of digital photographs showing views from the different windows around school. If the photographs were numbered, the children could be asked to identify each of the different views and from which rooms the photographs were taken.

Crossing Carefully

Equipment Needed

Dark coloured sugar paper e.g. olive green, brown or dark blue A4 size. Oil pastel crayons, A4 and A5 pieces of card or stiff paper in various colours, scissors, glue, paper clips and photographs of the local crossing patrol i.e. the lollipop man or lady.

Talk About

*   The traffic they see on the way to school and where they think it is going.
*   Where traffic parks outside school and inside the school grounds.
*   The signs that tell traffic where the school is, where not to park etc. and why those signs are there. Where it is safe to cross the road and where it is not.
*   How and when the crossing patrol is there to stop the traffic.
*   The uniform worn by the crossing patrol.
*   Who uses the crossing patrol and what the lollipop man or lady is called.
*   Drawing with oil pastel crayons on dark coloured paper. How they are soft, brightly coloured and break easily.
*   Rolling card into a tube and fastening it together using paper clips.
*   Tearing stiff paper and card into shapes and strips and sticking these pieces on to a tube.

Doing

*   Get a piece of sugar paper and some oil pastel crayons. Arrange the paper portrait style. Look carefully at the photographs of the crossing patrol to find the colours that match for your drawing. Sketch with your finger first the outline of the crossing patrol person to get an idea of the size it will need to be on the paper, before drawing and colouring it in. Add traffic or children to your picture as well if you wish.
*   Make a 3D model of either a crossing patrol person or a person wanting to cross the road by getting a piece of A4 card, rolling it into a tube and fastening it together both at the top and bottom with paper clips.
*   Tear a circle of paper as a face, draw or tear and stick features on to the face before attaching it to the front of the top of the tube.
*   Tear strips for arms and attach these to the back of the tube before curving them round to the front and sticking them down.
*   Tear other shapes for hands and feet, skirts or trousers and stick them on to the front of the tube to complete the figure.
*   If you have made a crossing patrol person you will need to add the lollipop.

Display

Mount the drawings of the crossing patrol person individually and arrange them around the edge of photographs of traffic and traffic signs taken outside school. Arrange the 3D crossing patrol models on a flat surface beneath the display, each with a group of model people they are helping to cross the road plus model cars.

Parks and Gardens

Talking of Trees

Equipment Needed

Photographs of different types of trees at different times of the year i.e. some bare, some with green leaves, some with autumn leaves and some with blossom. Paint, paintbrushes, pieces of card to use as palettes, small pieces of sponge, small thin strips of card and pieces of white paper approx 30x30 cm plus scrap pieces of paper to practise on.

Talk About

- Why people plant trees in parks and gardens - to improve the environment and the view, hide ugly buildings, to reduce traffic noise, to give privacy, to provide fruit, to commemorate events etc.
- The types of trees in their own gardens, the locality and in the school grounds.
- The time of the year indicated by each of the trees in the pictures and why.
- Printing with a piece of sponge by pressing it on and lifting it off the paper rather than smearing and spreading with it.
- Printing lines with the edge of a piece of card dipped in paint, bending it to make curved lines and dragging it to make thicker ones.
- Drawing outline shapes with the edge of a brush and filling in the gaps between them carefully.

Doing

- Choose a picture of a tree to work from if it is not possible to go outside and sketch one.
- If the tree is going to have leaves or blossom on it get a piece of white paper, a piece of sponge and the colours of paint you need on a piece of card. Dip the sponge in the paint - use one colour at a time (for each dip) - and cover the paper with overlapping dabs of colour. Dab in colours for the trunk of the tree and the ground underneath it. When the paint is dry get a thin strip of card and some black paint. Dip the card in the paint and add linear

branches and a trunk to your tree. Some of the branches will be curved and some straight. Drag some thicker lines for the trunk. Allow some of the lines to touch and make others shorter as though they are pushing their way through foliage.

- If the tree is bare, as many trees are in winter time, mix some grey paint and on a piece of white paper. Carefully draw the outline of a tree and its branches. Make sure they are attached to the trunk but leave gaps between the branches. Make the branches thick near the trunk and thinner as they stretch upwards. Put cold colours of paint on a piece of card e.g. blues, purple and mauve and use these to fill in the gaps between the branches. Use greens and brown to fill in the gaps nearer the ground.

Display

Mount the pieces of work individually and display them in equally spaced rows around a central block of the photographs of actual trees.

Flowers and Flowerbeds

Equipment Needed

Brushes, paint, and pieces of card to put it on. White chalk, an assortment of coloured papers, cotton buds, thin strips of card, scissors and glue. Pieces 21x30 cm grey sugar paper for collage work and several pieces of A1 grey sugar paper taped together for large scale collaborative paintings. Pictures of park flower beds and gardens plus actual flowers for observational drawing.

Talk About

- Where the local parks are, what they are called and where they are on a map of the area. The flower beds in parks - how they are often full of the same variety and same colour of flowers planted in rows. Flower beds in gardens where there is more likely to be lots of different types of flowers in a variety of colours. Who looks after the flower beds in parks and who looks after the garden at home. That gardening can be a job as well as a leisure activity.
- How flower beds improve the environment, help us to appreciate the changing seasons, can be enjoyed by people without gardens, attract wildlife etc.
- The names of some of the different types of flowers planted in flower beds.
- Looking carefully at the shapes and colours of flower heads, leaves, stems.
- Printing with cotton buds and strips of card. Tearing and cutting shapes from different coloured papers and gluing them on to a background.
- Working together on a large - scale painting sharing the space.

Doing

- For a large scale painting, place the taped together pieces of paper on the floor. Ask children in the group who will be working on it to each choose the same type of flower from the collection to draw in their flower bed. Look at it carefully before starting to draw it in

white chalk in a fairly large scale on the background. Remind them to draw their flowers in rows as in a park flower bed. Each child in turn, will now need to paint their flower head in a shade of the same colour before adding green leaves and a stem. When these are dry any gaps can be filled with shades of green and brown.

- For a collage panel, each child needs to put their piece of paper portrait way up, tear strips of green tissue paper and stick them to fill the background touching and overlapping. The flowers are going to be imaginary and arranged as in a garden. Cut or tear flower heads or petal shapes and stick them in groups on top of the tissue paper. Add stems and details by printing with cotton buds and strips of card.

Display

The large scale painting will need a border strip around it once it is on the board to make it appear as though it has been mounted. The collages can be put together as a block again surrounded by a border strip. Display the pictures of gardens and parks looked at and discussed, alongside the display.

9

Birds, Bugs and Butterflies

Equipment Needed

Paint, pieces of card as palettes, thin strips of card, cotton buds, squares of grey sugar paper 25 x 25cm approx, scrap pieces to practise on. Black sugar paper A3 size or bigger, white chalk, scissors, silver, white and grey paper. White paper A4 size, oil pastels and wax crayons. Pictures of birds, butterflies and insects (actual specimens if possible on loan from a museum).

Talk About

• Shrubs and flowers that are planted in parks and gardens especially to attract insects, butterflies and birds as many species are in danger of extinction - what this means and why this might be. Why insects, birds and butterflies are important to the environment. The names and description of insects and birds they are familiar with and have seen in parks and gardens.
• Printing with cotton buds and strips of card. Cutting through both sides of a folded piece of paper to reveal a symmetrical design when opened.
• The shapes and body parts of the butterflies, birds and insects in the pictures and the colours and patterns on them.
• Drawing with wax crayons and oil pastels.

Doing

• Experiment on scrap paper with cotton buds and strips of card dipped in paint to discover the different types of marks you can print. Look at the insect pictures for ideas for body shapes, legs, etc. Your insect is going to be imaginary. On a square of grey paper use any colours you want and just strips of card, your fingers and cotton buds to make a picture of an insect by printing.
• For a butterfly, get a piece of black paper, fold it in half lengthwise. On one half, whilst it is

folded, draw the outline shape of half a butterfly in white chalk. Cut it out carefully, keeping the paper folded. Still with the paper folded, draw with white chalk patterns on both the top and bottom wings. Make the shapes in the patterns fairly big as they are going to be cut out with the paper still folded. When it is opened up you should have a symmetrically patterned butterfly. On the back where you can still see parts of your chalk lines, stick pieces of silver, grey and white papers so that they show through the shapes on the front. Use matching colours for identical shapes.
• Make observational drawings of birds in wax crayon or oil pastel using pictures or specimens as a stimulus.

Display

Arrange the butterflies as though flying at different angles across a brightly backed board. Mount the printed insects individually and arrange them as a block with pictures of actual insects as a border. Mount the bird drawings in a similar way.

Playground Possibilities

Equipment Needed

Coloured card A4 size (card thickness is ideal, stiff but easy to cut), drawing pencils (4b-6b), scissors, pictures of playground equipment in local parks plus a map of a local park.

Talk About

*   Who visits the local park - mothers with children, people walking dogs, people jogging etc, when they visit it and what there is for them to see and do there - places to sit, a café, a pond, a playground and which age group each of these amenities cater for.
*   What they would like to see as an addition to their local park and whom they would hope it would attract.
*   Rules necessary for safety and care of the environment and visitors to the park e.g. litter bins, warning notices etc.
*   What they can see in the playgrounds in the pictures. What play equipment they like to go on in the park and what sort of play equipment they or their friends have in their gardens.
*   Which of the play equipment is suitable for young children and which is for older children - and why.
*   The shapes and colours of the playground equipment - it is usually very brightly coloured.
*   Drawing shapes on coloured card and cutting them out.
*   Cutting slits in the shapes and slotting them together.

Doing

*   Choose some pieces of coloured card that match the colours of the playground

equipment in the pictures.
*   Get a drawing pencil, look carefully at some of the shapes of the playground equipment and draw some of these shapes on the different pieces of card. Make them fairly large as they are going to be cut out. They do not all have to be the same size.
*   Cut the pieces out carefully, cut short slits in each piece and by slotting the slits together begin building a new shape.
*   If it topples over, undo the pieces and slot them together in a different way until you have a stable structure that is abstract in design but based on the shapes of playground equipment.
*   If you feel your structure looks a bit unfinished or dull, draw and cut out some extra shapes that are different and slot these in for interest.

Display

Display the map of the local park with labelled pictures of the amenities in it. On a surface under the map covered in green paper, arrange the 3D structures based on playground equipment.

On the Beach

Equipment Needed

Tissue paper in assorted colours, glue and white paper A3 size. Chalk or chalk pastels in assorted colours, black or dark coloured sugar paper A3 size. Pictures of the seaside - travel brochures and postcards are a useful source.

Talk About

- Trips the children may have made to the seaside - how they got there, what the resort was called, what they saw and what they did whilst they were there.
- What they can see in the pictures of the seaside.
- Making a picture of the seaside using their own ideas and those in pictures.
- What they might include in a picture of the seaside.
- The colours they will need for the beach and for the sea.
- Tearing tissue paper into strips and shapes. How to stick them on a background - how much glue to use and where to put it.
- Allowing the shapes to touch and overlap to cover the background.
- Drawing with chalk or chalk pastel - how to smudge, spread and blend colour as well as to draw lines and shapes.
- Working from the top of the paper down so that the drawing doesn't become rubbed and spoiled.

Doing

- Decide whether your picture is going to be a drawing or a collage and get a piece of A3 paper as your background.
- Choose either tissue paper or chalk / chalk pastel to work with.
- Choose the colours of tissue paper for the sand and sea, tear them into small pieces

before sticking them in place to form the different parts of your picture.
- Now choose the colours for the people and other parts of your picture e.g. rocks, towels etc. Tear the shapes you need, arrange and then stick them on top of the sand or sea in your picture.
- If your work is a drawing, choose the colours you need for the sea and the sand and lightly, with the chalk / chalk pastel on its side, cover areas for the sand and the sea.
- Draw an outline of the shapes of the people and other things in your picture e.g. boats, sand castles etc. before filling them in by pressing down firmly with the chalk/ chalk pastels. Work at the top of the paper first, gradually moving downwards to avoid smudging.

Display

The chalk/ chalk pastel drawings will need fixing before they are mounted and put on display - spray a light covering of hair spray over each one. Mount each piece of work individually and arrange them in equally spaced rows - arrange the collages together on one side of the board and the drawings together on the other. Surround the display with 'seaside' words, e.g. sand, waves, shingle etc.

Shells as a Stimulus

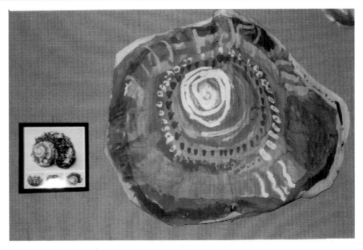

Equipment Needed

Grey sugar paper A3 size, paint, paintbrushes and pieces of card to use as mixing palettes. Pictures of different types of shells, actual shells and magnifying glasses to look at them more closely.

Talk About

- The different types of shells, those that are similar and those that are different.
- The different sizes of the shells.
- The outline shapes of the shells and the textures on them.
- Those shells that come from beaches in this country and those that have come from countries abroad.
- The colours and patterns on the shells.
- Drawing thick lines and thin lines with a paint brush.
- Drawing dots and shapes with a paintbrush.
- Mixing colours together to make new colours with a paintbrush on a piece of card.
- Painting, after looking carefully at a shell either its whole shape or just the pattern on it.
- Matching the colours and lines carefully but making the work larger than the actual shell so that it fills the whole of the paper.

Doing

- Put a shell in front of you and look at it carefully. Decide whether your work is going to be a picture of the shell itself or just the pattern on it.
- Get a piece of A3 paper and with your finger, draw either the shape of the shell or the pattern you can see - this will help you to find out how big your work will need to be to fill the paper.
- Get a paintbrush, a piece of card and a pale shade of paint e.g. grey and on your A3 paper draw either the outline of your shell or the main parts of the pattern on it.
- Now mix in turn the colours you can see on

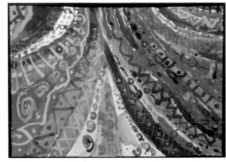

your shell and use them to fill and complete either your pattern or the shape of the shell.

- Once the paint is dry, draw in further details e.g. lines, dots and shapes with a brush to complete your work.

Display

Cut out the large shell paintings, put crumpled newspaper behind them as they are attached to the wall to pad them out and make them appear 3D. Include pictures of the shells the children looked at next to them and arrange the actual shells and magnifying glasses on a surface near to the display. Mount the shell patterns individually and display them together in equally spaced rows on a separate board near the display of actual shells.

Picking up Pebbles

Equipment Needed

Drawing pencils (4B-6B) pieces of white paper A4 size and pieces of scrap paper to practise on. Black and white chalk pastels and pieces of grey sugar paper A3 size and pieces of scrap paper to practise on. Clay cut into pebble sized chunks, reclaimed materials e.g. pegs, spatulas, bubble wrap etc. to press into the clay and paper towels to rest the clay on. A

collection of pebbles with interesting patterns on them and a bowl of water to dip them in to reveal their colours more vividly.

Talk About

- The type of materials that make up a beach - sand, shingle, pebbles, shells, rocks etc.
- The shapes and colours of the pebbles in the collection.
- The patterns and textures on the pebbles in the collection and how they feel to touch.
- The difference in the appearance of the pebbles when they are wet and when they are dry.
- Making light and dark grey with a pencil by pressing on gently and pressing on more firmly.
- Drawing with chalk pastels.
- Rolling clay into a ball and cutting and pressing into it using different reclaimed materials to make patterns and textures on it.

Doing

- Get either a drawing pencil and a scrap piece of white paper or black and white chalk pastels and a scrap of grey sugar paper and explore making light and dark patches (tones).
- Choose a pebble, dip it in water and look carefully at the pattern on it. Look for the darkest parts of the pattern, the lightest parts and the parts in between.

- On a new piece of paper use your pencil or chalk pastel to draw the outline shape of your pebble. By pressing on firmly and gently, use different shades of dark and light to fill in the shape and add a pattern to it.
- Draw several different pebbles in the same way.
- Get a piece of clay and put it on a paper towel. Roll it into a smooth ball shape. Look carefully at one of the pebbles and squash or stretch your clay ball to match its shape.
- Look at the patterns and textures on the pebble. Use the different reclaimed materials on the clay, pressing and drawing in it, to add patterns and textures like the original pebble.

Display

Mount the pebble drawings individually on black and display them in equally spaced rows on a grey background. Display the 3D pebbles on squares of black paper on a grey covered surface along with the real pebbles.

Going to the Seaside

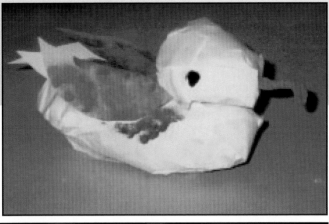

Seagull Shapes

Equipment Needed
White paper A3 and A4 size, circles of grey sugar paper, masking tape, scissors, glue and glue spreaders, orange pipe-cleaners, black and white paint, paintbrushes and pieces of card to put it on. Photographs of seagulls.

Talk About
- The birds that they see in the playground - are any of them gulls? Have they seen gulls before - if so where?
- The sizes of the birds in the playground and the size of the gulls in the pictures.
- Which is the biggest part of the bird and which is the smallest.
- The colours of the birds in the playground and the colours of the gulls in the pictures.
- How to crumple paper into a ball.
- How to tear masking tape into strips and then stick it on a surface.
- How to make grey paint by mixing a lot of white with very little black.
- How to bend a pipe-cleaner in half.

Doing
- Get a piece of white A3 paper and crumple it into a ball. Tear some strips of masking tape and use them to fasten the ball together.
- Get a piece of A4 white paper and crumple it into a ball. Tear some strips of masking tape and use them to fasten the ball together.
- Get some glue and a glue spreader and glue the smaller ball on top of and to the front of the larger ball. You have now made the head and body of your gull.
- Get a circle of grey sugar paper, fold it in half and then cut along the fold.
- Stick the two halves behind the head on either side of the top of the body as wings.

- Mix some grey paint on a palette and with a brush dab it on to the wings.
- Dip a finger in some black paint and print an eye on each side of the head.
- Bend an orange pipe-cleaner in half and poke the two ends into the front of the head - you may need an adult to help you with this. This is the gull's beak - bend the front of the beak slightly downwards.
- Now that your gull is complete make a drawing or a painting of it from observation.

Display
Mount the drawings and paintings of the gulls individually and arrange them in equally spaced rows on a blue background. Use the same blue to cover the surface beneath the display and on this arrange the 3D gulls as though they are bobbing on the water.

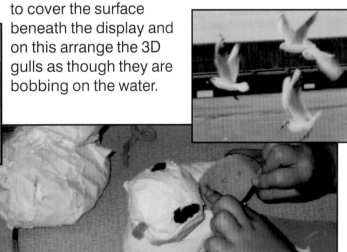

15

Starting with Stripes

Equipment Needed

Paint, brushes, pieces of card to put the paint on, pieces of white paper A4 size and 21cm x 21cm, scissors, wax crayons, drawing pencils, viewfinders, examples of striped patterns and a deckchair. Pictures of the seaside that include items with stripes on them.

Talk About

- What a striped pattern is. Striped patterns they can see in the room or on their clothes.
- Things they would take on an outing to the seaside which might have a striped pattern on them e.g. towels, swimsuits, buckets.
- Things they might see at the seaside with striped patterns on them e.g. wind breaks, awnings, beach huts, deckchairs etc.
- Using a different brush for each of the colours in a striped pattern so that the colours stay pure.
- Looking through a viewfinder and focussing on part of a deckchair only.
- Pressing on firmly with wax crayons for a rich covering of colour.

Doing

- Get a piece of white A4 paper, 2 paintbrushes and two different colours of paint on a piece of card.
- Decide which way the stripes are going to go on your paper and whether they are going to be thick or thin.
- Using each brush alternately, paint a striped pattern that fills your piece of paper.
- When the paint is dry decide what stripey item your pattern is going to be turned into. Draw the outline of it e.g. a beach hut on top of the pattern and cut it out. Use a paintbrush and a new colour of paint to add any extra details e.g. a door.
- Get a viewfinder, a drawing pencil and a piece of white (21 x 21cm) paper. Look carefully at

part of the deckchair through your viewfinder before drawing it on your piece of paper. Make your drawing large enough to fill all of your paper.

- Look at the colours of the deck chair and find them in wax crayons. Use these colours to fill in the shapes you have drawn. Press on firmly for a rich covering of colour.
- Further striped patterns could also be developed using the computer.

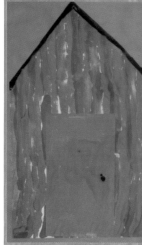

Display

Mount the individual stripey items and arrange them around the pictures of the seaside. Add a label to each one to describe it and what it is for. Put photographs of the deckchair and the children drawing it in the centre of another board. Individually mount the completed drawings and display them with equal but small spaces between them around the edge of the photographs.

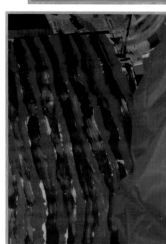

Terrific Tartan

Equipment Needed
A4 pieces of coloured card, coloured paper cut into both thick and thin strips, scissors and glue. A computer graphics program (Dazzle has been used here) and a printer. Examples of tartan.

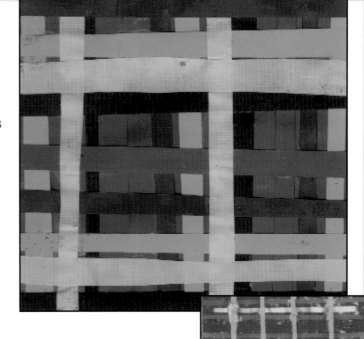

Talk About
*   What a tartan pattern looks like. The examples of different tartan patterns - what is similar about them and what is different. Tartan patterns they can see on their clothes, in the environment and in the illustrations of the stories about Katie Morag by Mairi Hedderwick. The story behind this pattern - Tartan is a specific woven pattern that signifies a particular Scottish clan. Tartan patterns have been used in Scottish weaving for centuries. Every clan has at least one distinct tartan, there is however no penalty attached to the wearing of tartans belonging to other clans. Tartans have been recently designed for commercial use, football clubs, cities etc. and the world of fashion.
*   Finding out more about tartan on the Internet.
*   Arranging strips of paper horizontally and vertically on a coloured background 'tartan style' and sticking them down. Putting thin strips on top of thick strips.
*   Weaving with strips of paper - starting with one strip horizontal and one vertical, making a cross. Adding further strips both horizontally and vertically, starting each in the opposite way to the previous strip i.e. either over or under depending on how the previous strip was woven.
*   Using the line tool, the fill tool and the grid tool on the computer to draw a pattern 'tartan style'. Where to find these tools, how to get them and how to alter the width of the line using the right - hand mouse button (See Step by Step Art 6 page 8).

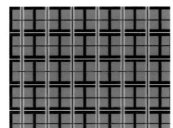

Doing
*   Get a piece of coloured card and some coloured strips of paper. Look carefully at the way the pattern of lines on the tartan overlap and repeat. Arrange your strips of paper in a similar way. Stick them to the background whilst keeping the pattern intact. Use both thick and thin strips.
*   Get some strips of coloured paper and following the instructions above, begin weaving them together. You will need to repeat the same sequence of colours several times to achieve a 'tartan style' pattern.
*   Using the grid tool, the line tool and different colours, draw a 'tartan style' pattern on the computer. Vary the thickness of the lines and try drawing thin lines on top of thick ones. Save and print out your design when it is finished.

Display
Mount the different types of work individually and display around the actual examples of tartan. Display other tartan items under the display.

Fabulous Fair Isle

Equipment Needed

A computer graphics program (Dazzle has been used here) a printer and examples of knitwear that has Fair Isle patterns on it. Also examples of Arran Knitwear and a map of the British Isles.

Talk About

- What a Fair Isle looks like. The examples of Fair Isle patterns. What is similar about them and what is different. Where they can see Fair Isle patterns in the illustrations of the stories of Katie Morag by Mairi Hedderwick.
- Where these patterns come from - Fair Isle patterns originate from the Shetland Islands (find these on the map). It is thought that the islanders developed their brightly coloured knitting to incorporate the symbols of their ancient religions in their knitted garments. It was common practice for a grandmother to knit the first sweater that her grandson would own as he reached adolescence - his robe of glory.
- The patterns on the Arran knitwear and who might have worn it in the Katie Morag stories. Such garments were/ are knitted from natural home-spun yarns from local sheep and either left in their natural colours or dyed with dyestuffs from local plants. The garments were/ are made up of stitch patterns that combine purl and plain stitches, twists and cables to represent the working environment and the life of a fisherman - the designs were originally developed by fisherfolk for protection from biting winds.
- The tools to use on the computer - the line tool, the grid tool, the square brush, the round brush and the fill tool - where to find them and how to get them.
- How to make the square brush and the round brush bigger and smaller and the line tool thicker and thinner using the right -hand mouse button - See Step by Step Art Book 6 pages 8 and 9.

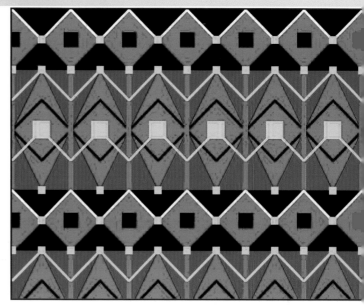

Doing

- Look carefully at the Fair Isle patterns before you start, the shapes and colours in them and how these are repeated and fit together.

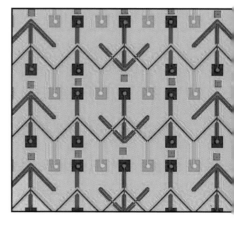

- Click on the grid tool and once it is on the screen use the line tool and the square and round brushes to draw your pattern. Use different line widths and the round and square brush in different sizes to make the pattern more interesting plus a range of bright colours.
- Save and print out your work when it is finished.

Display

Mount the pieces of work individually. Put a map of the British Isles that shows the Shetland Islands in the middle of the board and arrange the pieces of work around it. Display the actual examples of Fair Isle and Arran knitwear underneath the display.

A Scottish Island Home

Crofts and Castles

Equipment Needed
Pieces of A4 and A3 paper in green, blue and grey to use as a background. Different types of other coloured papers e.g. tissue, corrugated paper, sugar paper etc. glue, paint, pieces of card to put it on, thin strips of card and other reclaimed materials to print with, drawing pencils (4b-6b) and scrap pieces of paper to sketch on. Copies of Katie Morag storybooks by Mairi Hedderwick.

Talk About
* The names of the different types of buildings in the locality.
* The names of the different types of buildings on the Isle of Struay e.g. the castle, the shop and post office, the lighthouse, the hut etc. and what these buildings look like in the illustrations.
* Tearing paper into different shapes and sizes and arranging these shapes so they touch and overlap on a background before sticking them down - how much glue to use and where to put it.
* Printing different sorts of lines with thin strips of card.
* Printing different marks with the range of reclaimed materials.

Doing
* Choose the colour and size of background paper you want to use and which way up you want to put it - landscape or portrait.
* Decide which of the buildings on the Isle of Struay you want to make a picture of by looking at the storybooks - make a sketch of the building and add notes about colours, patterns, shapes, textures etc. that you see on it, behind it and in front of it.
* Choose the colours of papers that match your notes plus the sort of papers you feel match the texture of the building best.
* Tear from the pieces of paper the main

shapes of your building, arrange them on the background and when you are happy with your arrangement, stick them down.
* Now tear smaller shapes to add detail to your building e.g. doors, windows etc. You might want to use some smaller pieces in front or behind your building.
* Put some paint - probably black, white, green, brown and blue will be the most appropriate on a piece of card and dip strips of card and other reclaimed materials in paint and add printing for further detail to both your building and its setting.

Display
Mount the pictures individually - the children could write the name of their building on the computer as a label to go under their work. Photocopy the map of the Island of Struay and mount this to go in the middle of the board. Arrange the collages around the edge and attach each one with a piece of yarn to the building on the map that it is a picture of.

A Scottish Island Home

Models and Maps

Equipment Needed

Thick pieces of card approx 30cm square, newspaper, masking tape, modroc (plaster of paris on a bandage) brown, blue, white and green paint, pieces of card to put it on, brushes, squares of coloured paper, glue, strips of white paper approx 5cm wide. Books about Katie Morag by Mairi Hedderwick and maps that show the shapes of other islands.

Talk About

- The shape of the island of Struay as shown in the books.
- Finding other islands on the maps and describing their shape.
- Scrunching newspaper into large and small balls and taping the balls together with masking tape on to a card base.
- How to use modroc - by cutting it into strips, dipping a strip briefly into a bowl of water to allow it to become soft before draping it over and pressing it onto the surface to be covered. Then getting another strip and repeating the process. Continuing this way until all the surface is covered.
- The colours of paint to use and which part of the model they would be appropriate for e.g. cliffs or rocks, hills, lakes etc.

Doing

- You are going to make a model of an island. It could be the same shape as the Island of Struay, one of the islands found on the map, or completely imaginary. Get a thick square of card, newspaper and masking tape.
- Scrumple the newspaper into large and small parcels and use tape both to hold each one together and to fasten them to the square of card. Remember to allow some dips as valleys or lakes and make some parts higher as hills etc.
- When the shape is complete, get some modroc, cut it into strips and dip each strip in turn into water before draping it and pressing

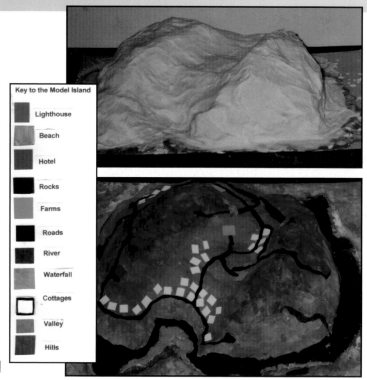

Key to the Model Island

	Lighthouse
	Beach
	Hotel
	Rocks
	Farms
	Roads
	River
	Waterfall
	Cottages
	Valley
	Hills

it on to and over the newspaper. Allow it to extend on to the base itself to hide the edges of the newspaper. When it is dry it needs to be painted. Get a brush, put some paint on a piece of card and paint your island and the sea around it. Decide where the different colours will be most appropriate. Get some coloured paper squares to represent the different buildings on your island. Use a different colour for each type of building - remember there may be several of some types e.g. cottages. On a strip of white paper stick a row of coloured squares that matches the colours you have used and next to each square write the name of the type of building it represents. This is the key to your model. You could draw a map of your island as well using wax crayons.

Display

Arrange the models on shelves attached to the board (see Step by Step Display in the Primary School page 28) with their keys next to them or on a flat surface under a board with maps of other islands including Struay on it.

Passport Pictures

Equipment Needed

Thin black felt tip pens, white paper A4 size, a Teddy bear, a real passport.

The outline of an actual passport page could be printed on the computer and the children's final drawings reduced in size using a photocopier and each one attached to a page for the children individually to complete.

Talk About

- What a passport is and why we need to have one.
- How to get a passport and where to get one from.
- How long a passport is valid.
- When to use a passport and why. Who looks at a passport and what happens to it on a visit to some countries (it gets stamped).
- The information that is shown on the page of a passport and what the cover looks like and what it says on it.
- That passports for the residents of other countries are different from ours i.e. the information in them will be much the same but the covers will be different.
- What the photographs on passports show - only the head and shoulders of a person - and the size these photographs need to be.
- Where you can have your passport photograph taken.
- The shapes seen on the teddy bear and how these shapes fit together.
- Which shapes are large and which shapes are small.
- Drawing with a black felt tip pen - remember it doesn't rub out!

Doing

- Put the teddy bear in front of you and look at it carefully.
- Look at the different shapes that make up its head and body and how these shapes fit together.
- You should really only draw its head for a passport picture - but we will break the rules!!!

- Get a piece of white paper and a black felt tip pen.
- Draw the shape of the bear - or just its head - on your piece of white paper with your finger to see how big you will need to make it to fill the paper.
- Now get a black felt tip pen and carefully draw the outline of the same shapes you drew before.
- Add his eyes, nose etc. and remember he must not be smiling - you are not supposed to smile on a passport photograph !

Display

Reduce the drawings in size and ask the children to stick them on the passport pages once they have completed them. Mount the original drawings individually and display them equally spaced in rows each with its matching passport page underneath. Cut pages out of travel brochures to use as a border around the edge of the display and display further brochures on a flat surface underneath it.

Suitcases and Souvenirs

Equipment Needed

The lids of A4 photocopying paper boxes or boxes of a similar size, brown paper and card, travel brochures, luggage labels, scissors, glue, strips of coloured paper approx 5 x 14 cm, a computer and a printer.

Talk About

- Souvenirs they have brought back from holidays both for themselves and as presents for other people. Making a collection of holiday souvenirs, looking at them and sorting them into souvenirs from places in this country and souvenirs from abroad.
- The names of the foreign countries from which the souvenirs from abroad have come and where these countries are on a map of the world.
- Making a class list of other types of souvenirs that the children can think of e.g. shells, jewellery, hats, brochures, tickets, coins etc.
- The sort of labels needed on luggage when people go on holiday - the owner's name and destination - and why these are necessary.
- Covering a box lid with brown paper. Cutting pictures out of travel brochures.
- Typing the name of Barnaby Bear and different countries using a variety of fonts on the computer.

Doing

- Get an A4 box lid and cover the outside of it with brown paper. Cut a handle shape out of brown card and stick it on the top of the box.
- Choose a font on the computer and in large letters write and print out the name Barnaby Bear. Cut the writing into a strip, stick it on a luggage label and tie the label on to the handle of your suitcase.
- Look at the names of different countries in travel brochures and on a map of the world. Decide which countries Barnaby Bear is going to take his suitcase to and type the names of these countries individually in different fonts using the computer. Each one will need to be fairly large and easily read. Print out the name of each country and cut them into individual strips. Stick the name of each country on to a separate coloured strip. Look in the travel brochures for a picture of somewhere or something from that country to cut out and stick next to its name. When the strips are completed stick them at angles on different parts of your box suitcase i.e. the outside of the box that has been covered with brown paper.

Display

Arrange the boxes in rows on the board around a map of the world - attach them to the board by fastening strips to each box so that they can be hung on the board. Display the collection of holiday souvenirs under the board together with the names of where they came from plus the children's list of suggested souvenirs.

Barnaby The Travelling Bear

Focus on Flags

Equipment Needed
Paint, pieces of card to put it on, paint brushes, wax crayons, coloured paper A4 size, white paper A4 size, scissors and glue plus pictures of the flags of different countries.

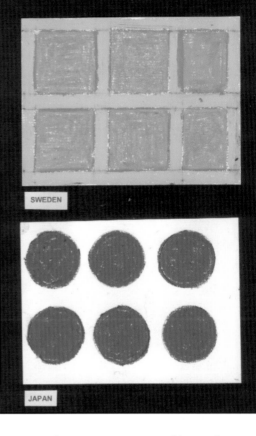

Talk About

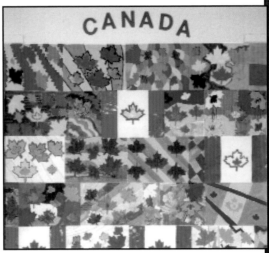

- That each country has its own National flag that is different from any other country.
- The name and design of the flag of this country and where and when this flag is flown.
- Other flags that the children are familiar with and where and when they have seen them flown e.g. the cross of St George appears on flags when English football supporters wish to show allegiance to their home team.
- The pictures of flags from different countries, the colours and patterns on them. Ask if there are any of them similar, if so how ?
- Finding the countries to which these flags belong on the map of the world.
- That Barnaby Bear would have seen different flags on his travels to other countries.
- Drawing lines and shapes with a paintbrush.
- Drawing lines and shapes with wax crayons.
- Cutting out different shapes from coloured paper and sticking them on to a background.
- How much glue to use and where to put it.

Doing
- Choose a picture of a flag from another country and look at the colours and shapes on it carefully and how they are arranged.
- You are going to design a new version of this flag using the same colours and shapes but arranging them in a different way.

- Get the colours of wax crayons and/or paint that match your flag and a piece of white paper.
- Decide on the background colours and the shapes you are going to use and cover and fill the white paper with them.
- Get the coloured paper that matches the original flag and decide which shapes you need to cut from it and add to your background. Arrange these shapes on the background and stick them down.
- Alternatively you could design a new flag for a country copying different versions of the shapes on the original flag and using a different set of colours.

Display
Arrange the flags, unmounted, in equally spaced rows and under each one write the name of the country it is intended for. At one side of the display or in the middle of it, put a map of the world and the pictures of the original flags. Attach each flag with a piece of yarn to the country it represents.

Holiday Snaps

Equipment Needed
Black felt tip pens, wax crayons, squares of white paper 6 x 6cm and 10 x 12 cm approx, travel brochures, scissors, glue and a teddy bear.

Talk About
- That people usually take photographs when they go on holiday and what these photographs usually show - interesting buildings, beaches, places they visited, places they stayed in, people they met etc.
- Could the children bring in some photographs of a family holiday and talk about them.
- Making some holiday snaps for Barnaby Bear.
- Drawing with a felt tip pen.
- Cutting out shapes from holiday brochures to make new pictures.
- Sticking these shapes on to a background - how much glue to use and where to put it.

Doing
- Get a small square of paper and a black felt tip pen.
- Put the teddy bear in front of you and look at its shape carefully and decide whether you are going to draw the bear as though it is standing up or sitting down.
- Draw it on the paper with your finger first to get an idea of the size it will need to be before drawing it in black felt tip pen.
- Your drawing will need copying several times - one for each holiday snap - using a photocopier.
- Now get a larger square of paper and some holiday brochures. Look through them to find and cut out shapes that will make up a picture as though it is a holiday snap. Colour in and add a sky using wax crayons - you may also need to choose and use other colours to fill in any gaps between the shapes.

- Cut out carefully one of the drawings of Barnaby Bear. Choose whether you want to leave it as a black outline or whether you want to colour it in before you arrange it and stick it on to your collage background.
- Make further holiday snaps in the same way using different picture parts and the photocopied drawings of Barnaby Bear.
- When people stick snaps in an album they often write a caption under each one. Ask the children to use the computer and write and print a caption for each of the Barnaby Bear holiday snaps they have made.

Display
Mount each holiday snap, along with its caption, individually and arrange them in equally spaced rows around the actual teddy bear they drew. Sit him on a shelf (See Step by Step Display in the Primary classroom page 28) in the middle of the board.

Signs on Shops

Equipment Needed

Pieces of white paper A4 size, glue, scissors, catalogues and magazines, pictures of local shops, a list of unusual shop names. Strips of white paper or coloured paper 30 cm x 6 cm, coloured felt tip pens, thin strips of black paper and rectangles of coloured paper to use as the shop doors.

Talk About

- The different types of shops in the local area or in a nearby town that are not supermarkets.
- What type of shop is a florist, a confectioners, a newsagent, opticians etc?
- Any shops with unusual names.
- Guessing the type of shops that match some of the names on the list e.g. The Crop Shop (a hairdressers)
- Cutting several similar items out of magazines and sticking them on to a background - how much glue to use and where to put it.
- Drawing the outline of letters with felt tip pens and then colouring them in or using the computer to print out letters in a chosen font and colour.

Doing

- Get a piece of white A4 paper and lay it landscape style in front of you.
- Choose a rectangle of coloured paper to stick at one side as the shop door.
- Decide what type of shop you are going to make a collage of - alternatively a list of different shop types could be cut into strips and the children asked to pick one and make the window display for that type of shop.
- Get a magazine or catalogue and cut out a collection of appropriate items for your shop window.
- Arrange them on the white paper to fill the space next to the door. When you are happy with your arrangement, stick it down.
- Get some strips of black paper and use them

to outline and divide up your shop window and outline the door.
- You now need to think of an unusual and appropriate name for your shop.
- Use felt tip pens to write the name (big and bold) on a strip of white or coloured paper or print out the name of your shop using a computer.
- This activity could be approached in other ways - each child could make a collage of a specific type of shop window before giving it to another child who needs to identify the type of shop and write out an appropriate name for it, or each child could be given the unusual name of a shop and asked to make a collage of an appropriate shop window to match it.

Display

Mount each shop together with its name on a black house shaped piece of paper. Arrange them in equally spaced rows across the board. Around the edge of the board could be the names of the different types of shops.

House Signs

Equipment Needed

An assortment of different types of coloured papers, scissors, glue, drawing pencils, felt tip pens and crayons, pieces of white and black paper A4 size, a computer and printer plus pictures of different house signs. A list of house names and a list of jobs and professions e.g. plumber, dentist, clockmaker etc. cut into strips.

Talk About

- The reason why houses have numbers and often names.
- Where the ideas for these names come from - a place the owners went on holiday, the position of the house, a combination of the owner's names etc.
- The names of their own houses, if they have them, and of houses in the locality.

- The sort of pictures found on house signs - they often match the name of the house in some way.
- The shape of the signs - usually oval, square or rectangular and where the lettering is placed.
- How to get different fonts and different sizes of fonts using the computer.
- Drawing with pencils, felt tips and wax crayons in order to be selective on later work. Cutting shapes out of the different papers and gluing them on to a background - how much glue to use and where to put it.

Doing

- From the cut up list choose a strip with either a name or a job on it - this will be the starting point for the design of your house sign.

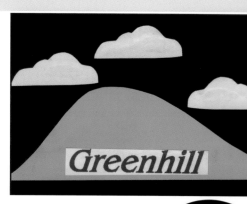

- Get a piece of either black or white A4 paper and cut it into the shape of your house sign.
- When you have sorted out the name of your house you will need to try printing it in different fonts of different sizes on the computer. When you are happy with your lettering, print it out. Remember it must fit on the shape you have cut for your house sign and leave room for a picture.

- Cut the printed lettering into strips and arrange it on your sign shape.
- Now get some coloured paper, decide what your picture is going to be of and begin cutting out the shapes you need for it from the coloured paper.
- Arrange the shapes on your sign shape. When you are happy with the arrangement, stick them down.
- Add further details to your picture by drawing either with pencil, felt tip pens or crayons.

Display

Back the board with coloured paper and on it put a large silhouette of a house shape cut from black paper. Arrange the house signs in equally spaced rows on this silhouette.

Local Attractions

Equipment Needed

Brown sugar paper cut into squares (15cm x 15cm), pieces of white paper, scrap pieces of paper to try out ideas on, scissors, glue, drawing pencils, a copy of the Highway Code and pictures of (brown) attraction signs plus a large scale map or aerial photograph of the local area.

Talk About

- What a silhouette is and what sort of attractions the silhouettes on the brown signs in the pictures are encouraging people to visit.
- Any brown signs that are already in the locality.
- The brown signs shown in the Highway Code.
- The map / aerial photograph of the local area and places/ attractions they think visitors to it need to know about e.g. football grounds, swimming pools, parks, playgrounds, canals, woods, monuments etc.
- Where these attractions are to be found/ are situated on the map/ aerial photograph of the local area.
- The silhouettes they might draw as signs for these attractions - remembering that they must be simple and easily recognisable.
- Drawing simple shapes on white paper and cutting the shapes out carefully.
- Sticking these shapes on to a background - how much glue to use and where to put it.

Doing

- Decide which local attraction you are going to make a sign for and on a scrap piece of paper sketch some ideas.
- It might be a good idea to discuss with the children the attraction they have chosen and offer suggestions so that there are not too many duplicates.

- When you have the idea you want to use, get a piece of brown paper and a piece of white paper.
- The silhouette you draw must fit on and almost fill the piece of brown paper.

- Sketch the shape of your silhouette carefully in pencil, put it next to your piece of brown paper to see if it is big enough - or too big - before cutting it out carefully and sticking it on to the brown square.

- Write (using the computer if you prefer) a brief description of the attraction on your sign and why it should be visited.

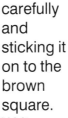
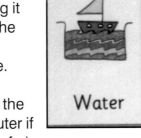

Display

When all the signs are complete ask the children in turn to hold up their signs for the rest of the class to identify the attraction they are showing. Put the map or the aerial photograph of the locality in the middle of the board and ask each child in turn to put the sign they have made (mounted on white) in the appropriate place on it - or on the edge of it with an arrow to the attraction. Mount the written descriptions on black and put them underneath each sign.

Signs and Symbols

Road Sign Symbols

Equipment Needed

An Ordnance Survey map of the locality, a copy of the Highway Code, pictures of roadside signs in the locality with symbols on them e.g. cycle track, school crossing, no entry etc. rather than words. A computer with a graphics programme and a printer (Dazzle has been used here).

Talk About

- What a symbol is and symbols on signs around school as well as written signs. What the Highway Code is and the symbols in it.
- What the symbols on the road signs mean- and how they can be understood if you are unable to read. Similarly such symbols help people to find their way around if they are visiting a foreign country and do not speak the language.
- The symbols they can find on the Ordnance Survey map and what they represent e.g. churches, telephone boxes, golf courses etc.
- The tools to use on the computer and how to get them - the fill tool, the shapes tools, the line tool, the text tool (how to change fonts and the size of the font), the select area tool and the tile/ tile and flip facility under Area on the top tool bar. For more help with these functions see the book Step by Step Art 6 - Working with the Computer.

Doing

- Decide which road sign symbol (choose a simple one) you are going to use for your design.
- E.g. For the roundabout design print in black a letter O from a font after clicking on the text box with the right - hand mouse button and selecting the size and type of font to use before clicking on close with the left - hand button.
- Click on the line tool and the colour white to cut the letter O into three separate pieces. Use red and the triangle shape to draw round the outside of the O using the left - hand

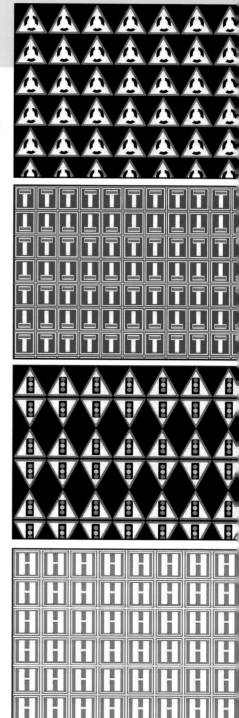

mouse button.
- Use the select square tool and the left hand mouse button to draw a box round the triangle.
- Go up to area on the top tool bar, and with the left hand mouse button drag down and click on tile. The screen should now be full of a repeat pattern of triangles.
- Use the fill tool, the colour black and the left hand mouse button to fill the gaps between the triangles.
- The traffic light sign has been done in a similar way but instead of tile, tile and flip has been used.
- Experiment with designs using other road sign symbols as a starting point.

Display

Mount the computer print outs individually and display them around a block of pictures of road signs taken from the Highway Code and in the locality.

A Symbolic Journey

Equipment Needed

Travel brochures, scissors, glue, drawing pencils (4b-6b), strips of white paper 30cm long x 12cm wide, paint, brushes, pieces of card to use as palettes, and pieces of A3 grey or cream sugar paper.

Talk About

- Symbols seen on maps and road signs and what they represent.
- How they are simple and easy to recognise.
- Cutting environmental features out of magazines e.g. beaches, forests, lakes, deserts etc. rather than pictures of people.
- Sticking them in a sequence along a strip of paper leaving a gap underneath the pictures.
- Drawing simple symbols. Painting the same symbols on a larger scale in a variety of colours, not in sequence and repeating the same symbol more than once.

Over the sea	Across a Beach	Through a forest	Up a mountain	and into a desert

Doing

- Get a strip of white paper, some scissors and some travel brochures. You are going to create an imaginary journey in pictures along your strip of paper using images cut out of the travel brochures.
- When you have a collection of the images you want to use, arrange them in sequence across your strip of paper with a gap underneath and stick them down.
- Now get a drawing pencil and under each picture draw a simple symbol to represent it.
- You are now going to use these symbols in a painting. Choose the colours of paint you want to use and put them on a card palette.

Get a brush and a piece of A3 paper.

- Use a pale shade of paint first e.g. grey to draw your symbols - fairly large - on different parts of your paper. You can repeat the same symbol more than once and draw smaller versions of the large ones in between the others.
- Use the different colours of paint you have chosen to work on top of your drawings and fill in any gaps between them with blocks of colour. The aim is to fill the paper completely with symbols relating to your journey in a wealth of colour

Display

Mount the journey paintings and initial collages individually. Display the paintings in equally spaced rows across the board and either arrange each collage under its matching painting or as a border around the edge of the board. The children could write descriptions of their imaginary journeys and where they went for display on a separate board.

29

Shapes from the Streets

Equipment Needed

Drawing pencils (4b-6b), wax crayons, pieces of grey sugar paper approx 17 x 17 cm, square viewfinders. It is helpful if the shape of the viewfinders the children use match the shape of the paper they are working on. A detailed map/plan of a local town that shows the outline of roads and the shapes of buildings along each one.

Talk About

- The shape of the road they live on - is it straight or curved, is there a roundabout or road junction on it, do other roads lead off it etc.
- What sort of buildings are there along the road?
- What can be seen on the map and what the different shapes on it represent.
- Where there are interesting shapes made by the roads and buildings.
- Using a viewfinder to select and isolate an area on the map.
- Drawing the outline of the shapes that can be seen through the viewfinder gently using a pencil.
- Colouring inside the drawn shapes carefully.
- Pressing on firmly with a wax crayon for a rich covering of colour.

Doing

- Place a viewfinder on the map and move it around until you can see an interesting collection of shapes in it.
- Get a piece of grey paper and a drawing pencil and make a rough outline sketch of what you can see through the viewfinder (some shapes will be large some small, some narrow, some wide etc.) and how they all fit together along the roads.
- If there are a lot of similar sized buildings close together don't count them for an exact match, just draw several in a group.

- Draw all the shapes larger than they actually are as they need to fill the paper.
- Get some wax crayons (any colours that you want) and begin to colour in the shapes you have drawn.
- Colour carefully within the shapes and press on firmly for a rich covering of colour.
- Add outlines to the shapes using the wax crayons if you feel they need it.

Display

Either: Put the wax crayon shape drawings together as a group to make a colourful abstract surrounded by a border of viewfinders and photographs of the children working.
Or: Mount the work individually and display around the edge of the map/plan the children looked at. Attach each one with a strip of coloured paper to viewfinders placed on the parts of the map that were used as a stimulus.

Making Use of Maps

Where in the World?

Equipment Needed
A map of the world with the countries filled in with different colours, drawing pencils, wax crayons, several copies of each of the letters in the alphabet, pieces of white paper 13x10 cm with 6 times 3cm squares drawn on it and a border of 2cm round the edge, a computer and a printer.

Talk About
- The names of countries in the world that the children know.
- The names of countries they have visited and where they are on the map.
- The names of some of the other countries on the world map.
- What an initial letter is.
- The initial letters of the names of some of the countries on the world map.
- The colours of some of the countries on the world map.
- Matching a letter of the alphabet to the initial letter of a country.
- Colouring with wax crayons, pressing on firmly for a rich covering of colour.
- Colouring inside the squares only and not on the borders.

Doing
- Put the letters of the alphabet upside down in a box in the middle of the table.
- Put the map of the world in a prominent place.
- Each child needs a square of paper, some wax crayons and a drawing pencil.
- Each child in turn selects a letter of the alphabet, then tries to find a country on the world map that starts with that letter.
- Once a country has been found, the colour used for that country has to be found in wax crayon and a square on the paper coloured in.
- Press on firmly for a rich covering of colour taking care to keep within the boundaries of the square.

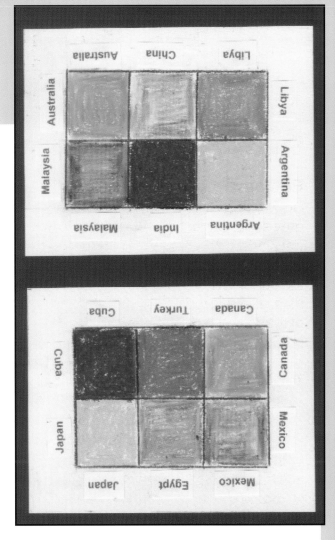

- The name of the 'found' country can be written in pencil next to the coloured-in square.
- The children continue choosing letters, finding countries and colouring squares until their piece of paper is filled. If a match cannot be found with a letter then the child has another turn.
- If the children find letters that match consecutively with countries that are the same colour encourage them to colour in where possible squares that are not adjacent to each other.

Display
Put the completed coloured squares together as a block surrounded by a narrow strip of paper and a wider border of coloured paper. Ask the children to write out in black and print out a list of the names of the countries they found for their square. Use these lists as a border around the edge of the block. Put a globe and the box of letters on a flat surface under the display.

Concentrating on Contours

Equipment Needed

Drawing pencils, (4b-6b) thin wax crayons, maps with interesting collections of contour lines on them e.g. hills and mountains, pieces of white paper 15 x 15 cm approx.

Talk About

- Is the country-side in the locality flat or are there any hills in the area ?
- How would these be shown on a map - by contour lines.
- Finding contour lines on a map of the local area.
- Finding contour lines on the other maps.
- The shapes made by contour lines.
- What it means if contour lines are close together and what it means if they are further apart.
- What the numbers next to contour lines mean.
- Drawing with pencils and wax crayons.
- Pressing on firmly when using crayons for a rich covering of colour.

Doing

- You are going to draw a pattern based on the shape and arrangement of contour lines somewhere on one of the maps.
- Get a drawing pencil and a square of white paper.
- Look carefully at the shape of the contour lines on one of the maps, follow the lines with your finger to find an interesting shape as the starting point for your pattern.
- Draw this shape, smaller than it actually is in the middle of the paper.
- Keep drawing round this shape until you reach the edge of your paper.
- As you draw round it you may want to alter the shape slightly and to change the size of the gaps between the lines in some places i.e. draw some of the lines closer together in parts similar to the way they appear on a map.

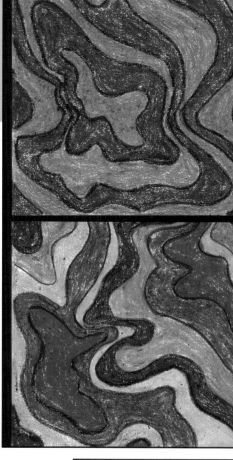

- Once this drawing is complete, a photocopy needs to be taken of it so that a second version can now be worked on. Using the thin wax crayons and any colours you want, carefully colour in the gaps between the lines.
- You might want to use a different colour for each ring of your drawing or to work using few colours, repeating them at regular intervals.
- Press on firmly as you work for a rich covering of colour.

Display

Arrange the pencil drawn contour line patterns as a block on a black background. Surround the block with a thin strip of grey. Arrange the coloured contour line patterns as a second block on the same black background. Surround this block with a thin strip of grey also. Photocopies of the parts of the maps showing interesting arrangements of contour lines could be photocopied, cut into strips and used as a border around the whole display.

Making Use of Maps

Town Trails

Equipment Needed

Drawing pencils (4b-6b) and wax crayons, pieces of white paper A4 size and smaller pieces 6 x 6cm. A map of the local area plus pictures of any interesting sights/ buildings that can be seen on a walk through it - alternatively a map of the local area around the school could be made on a board using strips of paper. Print the street / road names using the computer and add them to the map. A copy of the Highway Code.

Talk About

- The map of the local area, where the school is on it and where they live.
- The names of the different streets/roads on the map.
- The pictures of sights/buildings in the local area and where they should be placed on or alongside the map in the appropriate place.
- Symbols on traffic signs that give us e.g. directions of where to go (turn left, turn right etc). They are always simple and easy to understand.
- Writing down the route of a walk through the locality using the map. Sights to look at e.g. (look up at a church spire) are going to be suggested. Symbols are going to later be drawn for the instructions and a key to these symbols added.
- What a key on a map is, where it is likely to be found and what it shows.

Doing

- Look at the position of the school on the map, this is the starting point for your walk. Begin by writing down whether you turn left or right as you leave the school, where you go next, the name of the roads you go down, which direction to go and the sights to look at along the way.
- A walk might read something like this - Turn right into Green Lane, half way down the road, look up at the chimneys on the two old

cottages opposite. When you reach Church Road, turn right, stop just past the church, look and listen for traffic before crossing the road into Church View Terrace etc.

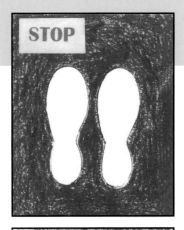

- Once your trail is written in pencil (and it has returned you to school!) put a ring round the written instructions you could draw symbols for. Make sketches of symbols you might use at the bottom of your paper - remember to keep them simple and easy to understand.

- Get some small squares of paper and one colour of wax crayon. Draw each of the symbols for your walk in pencil on a square of paper and colour in the background round it with the colour of wax crayon you have chosen.
- Write your walk out again sticking the symbols in the places where they replace words. Add a key i.e. draw a version of each symbol and write next to it what it means.

Display

Mount each walk individually and display them around a map of the locality. Alternatively, display in equally spaced rows with the map on a flat surface beneath.

Brick and Paving Patterns

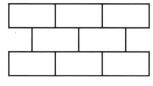

Equipment Needed

Red and black paint, pieces of card to use as palettes, white paper A4 size and 16 x 16 cm, old plasticene, thin strips of card, drawing pencils and pieces of scrap paper for initial sketches. A computer with a graphics programme (Dazzle has been used here). Pictures of both brick and paving patterns.

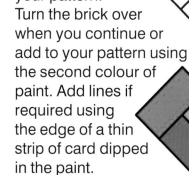

Talk About

- The patterns seen in brickwork and the way the shapes fit together.
- The patterns seen in paving and the way the shapes fit together.
- Where examples of these different patterns can be seen in the built environment and the colours seen in these patterns.
- Making brick shapes out of plasticene.
- How to print, by dipping one side of the brick shape into the paint, pressing it on to the paper and lifting it off before printing a second and further shapes the same way. Also printing lines with the edge of a piece of card dipped in paint
- Using opposite sides of the brick shape for each colour of paint.
- The tools to use on the computer - the line tool and the grid tool - where to find them and how to get them. Plus using the fill tool and appropriate colours to complete the drawing.

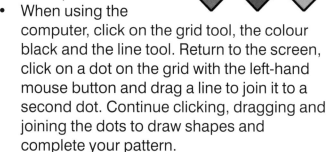

Doing

- Get a scrap piece of paper and a drawing pencil and make quick sketches of some of the brick and paving patterns you have seen or can see.
- Put some red and black paint on a card palette.
- Get a piece of plasticene and make it into a small brick shape.
- Look carefully at the brick and paving patterns you have drawn and choose one to copy. Get a piece of white paper of the

shape and size you want, dip the plasticene brick into the first colour of paint and begin printing your pattern.

- Turn the brick over when you continue or add to your pattern using the second colour of paint. Add lines if required using the edge of a thin strip of card dipped in the paint.

- When using the computer, click on the grid tool, the colour black and the line tool. Return to the screen, click on a dot on the grid with the left-hand mouse button and drag a line to join it to a second dot. Continue clicking, dragging and joining the dots to draw shapes and complete your pattern.

- Click on the grid to remove it from the screen, click on the fill tool, then the colour you want to fill the first shape before clicking inside the shape itself - all with the left hand mouse button. Fill the rest of the pattern with appropriate colours in the same way.

Display

Mount the pieces of work individually and arrange them in equally spaced rows. Put the computer work together in separate rows from the prints.

Windows and Doors

Equipment Needed

Black felt tip pens, white paper or card A4 size, thick and thin strips of black paper, pieces of black paper, circular shapes to draw round, scissors and glue. Washing powder boxes, white newsprint paper, drawing pencils and scrap pieces of paper, masking tape, paint, brushes, pieces of card to use as palettes and assorted reclaimed materials. Pictures of different types of doors and windows in public buildings, shops, offices and houses in a local town.

Talk About

- The shape, colour and design of the front door and windows on their own house and the different types of doors and windows on the houses, shops and buildings they pass on the way to school, in the local town and in the pictures.
- Cutting the strips of paper into pieces of equal length. Drawing round shapes and cutting them out. Folding a circular piece of paper in half and making a cut following the outer edge to take the centre out of it. Sticking the pieces of paper on to a background - how much glue to use and where to put it.
- Covering a washing powder box with newsprint - folding the newsprint over the edges of the box and taping it down with masking tape.
- The range of reclaimed materials available to turn the box into a doorway - and the sort of doorway it might be.

Doing

- Get a black felt tip pen and a piece of white paper or card and draw the outline shapes of some of the windows you see in the pictures or on your way to school.
- Get some strips of black paper, some round

shapes, scissors and glue and on a new piece of white paper design some new window shapes of your own using your drawings as a starting point. Stick the shapes down carefully. Make some windows very grand and some very simple.

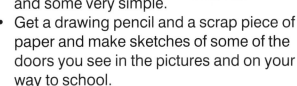

- Get a drawing pencil and a scrap piece of paper and make sketches of some of the doors you see in the pictures and on your way to school.
- Get a washing powder box and cover it with white newsprint - fold it over the corners and edges carefully and fasten it to the back of the box with masking tape. Use your sketches for ideas to design and make a door on the front of your box. Decide what colour the box needs to be painted, what shape your doorway is going to be, which materials you are going to use and how it might be decorated (e.g. with printing) before starting work on your box.

Display

Arrange the window collages as an unmounted block surrounded by pictures of windows in the local built environment. Fasten two strips of paper to the back of each 3D door and attach them in equally spaced rows across a display board.

The Built Environment

Gates and Railings

Equipment Needed

Drawing pencils and pieces of scrap paper for initial sketches, thick and thin strips of black paper, scissors and glue, pieces of white card A4 size. A computer with a graphics program (Dazzle has been used here). Pictures of gates and railings in the locality and in a local town.

Talk About

- Where gates and railings can be seen in the locality and in a local town.
- The materials they are made of and the different types of patterns on them.
- How to bend and curl strips of paper around a pencil.
- Sticking the strips of paper on their side in low relief instead of flat.
- How much glue to use and where to put it (i.e. on the background paper) before pressing the edge of the strips of paper on to it.
- The tools to use on the computer - where to find them and how to get them.
- How patterns are repeated in the designs of a run of railings.

Doing

- Get a drawing pencil and a scrap piece of paper and make sketches of some of the patterns found on the gates both in the locality and in the pictures.
- Decide what shapes and patterns to use in the design for a new gate.
- Explore cutting and folding the strips of black paper into these shapes.
- Arrange these shapes on a piece of white card in the way that you want them for your design and the pattern on it. Remember to stick gate posts on either side of your gate. These may be thicker than the actual gate itself and will be stuck down

flat rather than in relief.

- When you are happy with the arrangement put some glue on to the white card under the shapes and press the edges of them on to it carefully. You may need to press and hold them on for a while until the glue sets.

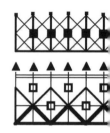

- On the computer find and use the grid tool, the line tool, the square shape and the circle shape by clicking on them with the left - hand mouse button.

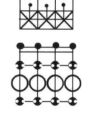

- Explore making both the square brush and the round brush smaller by clicking on them with the right - hand mouse button and then clicking on the ▼ in the box that appears using the left-hand mouse button. Click on close with the left - hand button when the brush is the required size.
- Combine and use these tools together in different ways to create new designs of repeating patterns for railings. The grid tool will help you keep each design in straight rows like the railings themselves.
- Use black for all the drawing.

Display

Mount each gate design individually on black and arrange them in a block touching each other in the middle of the board. Arrange the railing designs also mounted on black as a border around the edge of the display.

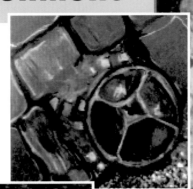

Looking Up and Looking Down

Equipment Needed

Large cardboard tubes, newspaper, modroc, paint, brushes, pieces of card to use as palettes, clay, squares of firm card 25 x 25 cm, scissors, glue, masking tape, coloured paper and card, drawing pencils, paper for initial sketches, viewfinders and assorted reclaimed materials.

Pictures of chimneys and different floorscapes.

Talk About

- The different shapes of the chimneys the children can see on houses in the built environment or in the pictures.
- Houses that don't have chimneys - and why.
- What a floorscape is and what might be seen on a floorscape in the built environment e.g. yellow lines, the edges of a pavement etc.
- Making quick sketches of both chimneys and a floorscape.
- Using a viewfinder to select the floorscape area to be drawn.
- How to crumple and fold newspaper into rolls, balls and pointed shapes, and how to stick these shapes on to a cardboard tube with masking tape or glue.
- How to use modroc - by dipping a small cut strip of it into water to soften it before wrapping it round and over the shapes on the tube.
- How to roll clay into sausages. How to coil these sausages into a spiral to make a base on which to build a coil pot with further sausages.
- How to smooth and pinch the coil pot to turn it into a chimney pot.
- The range of reclaimed material to be used for a floorscape and the card base to make it on.

Doing

- Get a drawing pencil, a piece of white paper and viewfinder. Either by looking up, or by looking at pictures, make quick sketches of several chimney pots.
- Decide which chimney pot you are going to build and the materials you are going to use i.e. clay or modroc, cardboard rolls and newspaper.
- Mix the colour of paint you need on a card palette and add colour to your finished chimney pot.
- Use a viewfinder to select your floorscape either by looking down or by selecting part of a picture of a floorscape. Make notes about the colours and textures you see on your sketches.
- Get a piece of thick card to use as a base and use the reclaimed materials to make your floorscape. Arrange the materials until you are happy with them before sticking them down. You may need to crumple, cut and colour some of the materials to achieve the effect you want.

Display

Arrange the floorscapes in rows with equal spaces between them on a display board under the heading 'Floorscapes'.
Arrange the chimney pots together with photographs on a flat surface.

Fitting Together

Equipment Needed

Drawing pencils and pieces of paper for initial sketching. Strips of white paper (approx 10 cm wide), scissors and glue. Small cut out b/w pictures of individual houses or shops from magazines. Pictures of shops, houses and other buildings that are joined to form a row in a local town. A range of coloured paper and A3 sheets of grey sugar paper if the work is to be extended into collaborative large scale work at a later stage.

Talk About

- Where rows of buildings that are joined together can found or seen in the local environment and in a local town What type of buildings these are and why they have been built close together e.g. a shopping precinct.
- The shape, size and colour of the buildings, the design of the doors and the windows etc. Those in a row that are identical and those that are not. Those that are old and those that are more modern - how can you tell? Why has this happened ?
- Sticking a black and white magazine picture of a house or shop in the middle of a strip of paper and drawing similar houses or shops on either side of it to make a row.
- Sketching the pattern of roof tiles and bricks on rough paper. Shading i.e. making light and dark grey with a pencil to add interest to the different houses.
- Choosing colours and cutting out door and window shapes if the work is later going to become a collaborative large scale collage.

Doing

- Get a strip of white paper and a b/w magazine picture of a house or shop. Stick it in the middle of your strip of white paper. Decide the sort of houses or shops you are going to add either side of your magazine picture. Draw the outline of each one before adding shading, and details such as tiles, bricks, window shapes etc.
- All the buildings do not need to be the same height or completely identical - look at the pictures of joined up buildings in the local town.
- Continue your row of buildings until it reaches the edges of your paper.
- This work could be developed as large scale collages of individual buildings as seen in the pictures of the local town and then later combined to form a row when they are displayed.
- Shapes, colours etc. of the building to be copied will need group discussion before shapes are cut out and arranged and stuck on grey sugar paper.

Display

The drawn rows of houses could be used as a border around written work about the built environment. The large scale collages could be arranged as a row with written work about the function of each building underneath.

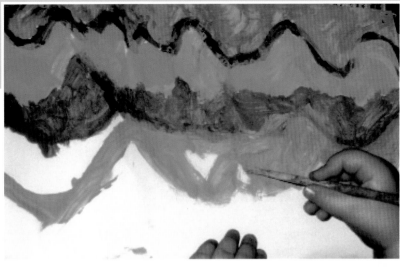

Fields of Green

Equipment Needed

Paint, brushes, pieces of card to use as mixing palettes, squares of grey or cream sugar paper 20cm x 20cm and pieces of A4 white paper. Paint shade cards showing different shades of green and aerial photographs showing green fields and the countryside, plus some that show views of the built environment for comparison. Pictures of fields taken at ground level.

Talk About

- What can be seen in the aerial photographs of the countryside and what can be seen in those of towns. What is similar and what is different.
- The pattern made by the fields fitting together - a patchwork.
- The different shades of green in the photographs and what they are e.g. woods, gardens etc.
- Naming and describing the different shades of green on the paint shade cards.
- How to mix green - blue and yellow - and how to make a variety of greens by adding different colours to green e.g. black, white etc. Naming and describing the different shades of green.
- Making a pattern using different shades of green.
- Making a pattern using different lines and shapes.
- What can be seen in the ground level pictures of the countryside - what is similar and what is different to the aerial pictures.

Doing

- Get a piece of card and a paint brush. Put some yellow and blue paint on the card and mix it together to make green.
- Get a square of sugar paper and on it begin painting a pattern using the green you have made.

- Add another colour to your green to alter it slightly - it 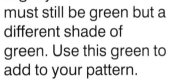 must still be green but a different shade of green. Use this green to add to your pattern.
- Mix further shades of green and use them as well until your pattern is complete. You may want to use some of the shades of green more than once.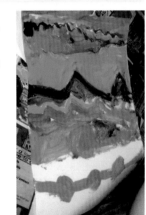
- As a further activity, get a piece of white paper and place it landscape style. Use the shades of green plus yellow, brown and blue to draw with a brush and fill in a picture of fields as though you are on the ground. Use the photographs to help you.

Display

Arrange the green patterned squares as an unmounted block on one side of a board - each square touching its neighbour. Put the aerial photographs of fields to one side of the block to show what the stimulus for the work was. Print the names the children gave to the different shades of green they have made and use them as a border around the edge of the display.

Cottage Colours

Equipment Needed

Paint, brushes, pieces of card to use as palettes, viewfinders, drawing pencils, white paper for initial sketches, oil pastel crayons, pieces of grey sugar paper A4 size and pictures of cottages in a country setting (calendars and travel brochures are a good source for these).

Talk About

- The colours of the cottages in the pictures - they are often painted in pastel colours - and what some cottages are made of - this may be of local stone as opposed to brick, and how they differ from houses in the built environment.
- The size and shape of the cottages, their doors, windows and gardens.
- Do they have garages? If not, why not?
- Looking carefully at the shape and colour of part of a cottage using a viewfinder - this could be done from first hand observation on a visit or from a picture.
- Making a quick sketch of part of a cottage and colour notes to use for final work.
- Mixing paint to make the colours noted on the sketch.
- Printing (dabbing) as well as making flat strokes with a paint brush to achieve different textures. Adding detail by drawing once the paint is dry.
- The colour and design of an imaginary country cottage.

Doing

- Get a piece of A4 grey sugar paper and arrange it portrait way up.
- With a paint brush and a pale shade of paint (grey) or a pencil, outline the main shapes similar to those you drew in your quick sketch.
- Get a paint brush, a card palette, and some paint and begin mixing the colours to match the stonework seen on your cottage - the

notes on your quick sketch should help you here.
- Use the brush in different ways, dabbing, stroking and drawing to add texture to the stonework. Outline and draw in further details once the paint is dry using oil pastel crayons.
- Alternatively, paint a picture of an imaginary cottage in a country setting on A3 grey sugar paper using information re colour, shape and setting etc. from pictures. Outline the main shapes first in a pale colour before filling them in. Once the paint is dry add further details using oil pastel crayons.

Display

Mount the colour matched cottages individually and display them with the initial sketches and colour notes around a block of photographs of stone built cottages.

Mount the imaginary cottages individually and display them as a border around colourful cottages found in calendars and magazines or in rows above written work describing these imaginary cottages.

Churches and Churchyards

Equipment Needed

Black handwriting pens or biros, oil pastel crayons, paint, brushes and pieces of card to use as palettes. Grey sugar paper A3 size, white paper A4 size, a computer with a graphics package (Dazzle has been used here). Pictures of country churches and church yards.

Talk About

*   The types of buildings found in a town and those found in a village. What is similar and what is different? The buildings that are the centre of village life - shops, schools, churches, village halls etc.
*   Village churches are in some cases quite small and in others quite large and imposing. They are full of dates and history about families who lived in the village in the past and possibly still live there. Churchyards also provide information about the village as do parish registers. Forthcoming events and village activities are often advertised in the porch of a church.
*   The names of churches in their locality and those noted in pictures or seen on a school visit. The shape of church buildings, towers, windows, porches etc.The shape and design of monuments in a churchyard. Drawing outline shapes with a handwriting pen, biro or paint brush. Filling in shapes and then adding details using oil pastel crayons.
*   The tools to use when drawing crosses on the computer, where to find them and how to get them.

Doing

*   Make a sketch of a view of a church on A4 white paper, portrait way up using a biro or black handwriting pen. Work either from observation or from a picture. Alternatively, on a piece of grey sugar paper A3 size, portrait way up, draw with a paint brush and pale shade, paint the outline of a view of a

church - work from a sketch made on a visit or from a picture. Fill in the shapes you have drawn with any colours you choose and draw in final details later using oil pastels.

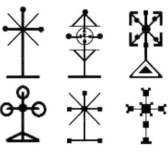

*   Using a painting package on the computer such as Dazzle, click on the grid tool then click on the line tool with the left-hand mouse button and by joining up the dots in different ways design crosses as monuments for a churchyard. Click on the grid tool with the left-hand mouse button to remove it. Use the right hand mouse button to click on the square brush and reduce it in size using the ▼ that appears in the box. Click on close and use the new brush to add detail to your designs. Reduce and use the round brush in the same way.

Display

Use the mounted computer work and pen drawings as a border around written work about the church. Display the paintings individually mounted with equal spaces between them.

Farms and Farm Animals

Equipment Needed

Paper plates, assorted coloured papers, wool, glue, scissors, paint, brushes and pieces of card to use as palettes, wax crayons and pieces of white paper A4 size. Pictures of farm animals, farm buildings and tractors plus toy models of the same.

Talk About

- The names of the different farms found on a map of the countryside.
- The types of buildings found on a farm and what they are used for.
- The type of vehicles found on a farm.
- The type of crops grown on a farm and the type of animals found on a farm.
- Where and how the farmer sells his crops, milk and animals e.g. farm shop, local market etc.
- Drawing with wax crayon by pressing on firmly for a rich covering of colour.
- Tearing and cutting shapes out of coloured paper and sticking them on a background. How much glue to use and where to put it.
- Painting a paper plate before decorating it.

Doing

- Decide which farm animal's face your paper plate is going to become. Look carefully at a picture or model of this animal to help you choose the right colours of paint and paper to use.
- To make the cow, get a paper plate, put some black paint on a piece of card and use a brush to dab some patches of black on either side of the front of the plate.
- Tear two identical shapes from black paper as ears and stick them on either side of the top of the plate. Tear a large pink piece as the nose and two smaller pink pieces as the inside of the ears and stick them on.
- Cut two curved pieces out of white paper for the horns and two circles as the outside of the eyes. Stick these on. Cut smaller black circles for the nostrils and for the centre of the eyes. Add strips of wool between the horns.
- The other farm animals illustrated have been made in a similar way using different colours of paint and paper.
- Use the models of the animals or the tractor as a starting point for a picture e.g. of a farmer working in the fields or children looking over a fence at animals in a field etc.
- Draw them in wax crayon, outlining the main shapes in white first before filling them in and adding extra details. Remember to press on firmly for a rich covering of colour.

Display

The faces of the farm animals could be used as a border around either writing about a farm visit or around the individually mounted and equally spaced pictures of farms, fields and animals.

Dandelions and Daisies

Equipment Needed

A copy of the Country Code, oil pastel crayons, white chalk and pieces of grey sugar paper and black paper A4 size, scrap pieces of paper for initial work. Pictures of wild flowers in the countryside and cultivated flowers in gardens and actual daisies and dandelions and dandelion heads to draw from observation.

Talk About

- What the Country Code tells us to do and not to do when visiting the countryside e.g. leave no litter, leave livestock, crops and machinery alone, keep to public paths across farmland, fasten all gates, protect wildlife, plants and trees etc. Discuss new rules the children think appropriate.
- Which are the pictures of wild flowers and which flowers mainly grow in garden settings?
- The names of the different flowers.
- How some wild flowers now have a protection order on them e.g. bluebells and primroses etc. and what this means.
- Wild flowers also grow in open spaces in the built environment - where they are often classed as weeds.
- The colour, shape, texture and arrangement of petals or seed heads on the flowers to be drawn.
- The different drawing media to choose from and what they are like to draw with e.g. chalk smudges easily, oil pastel crayons can be blended together to make new colours.

Doing

- Choose the flower or seed head you are going to draw and look carefully at its shape and texture and the colours on it.
- Decide which drawing media you are going to use and on a scrap piece paper try making the colours you are going to need for your final work and also the lines and shapes you will need to draw and how they fit together.
- Get a piece of A4 paper either grey or black and place it landscape style.
- Your drawing needs to fill the paper so try drawing it first with your finger to get an idea of the size it needs to be before starting on your final work.
- If you have chosen chalk to draw with remember to work from the top of the paper down to avoid smudging.
- Chalk drawings need fixing with hairspray before they are mounted and put on display.

Display

Use the computer to type and print out a copy of the Country Code. Mount it and put it in the middle of the board. Mount the dandelion and daisy drawings individually and display them in rows or as a border around the edge of the print out of the Country Code. Include photographs of other wild flowers if desired.

Under and Over - Eddies and Swirls

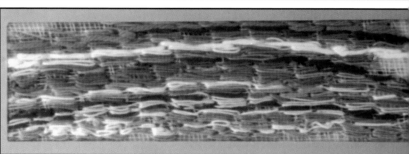

Equipment Needed

Coloured chalks or chalk pastels, grey sugar paper A4 size or cut into circles, blue, white and silver paper, blue foil, scissors and glue. Open weave fabric e.g. scrim or sequin waste cut into strips. Embroidery threads and thin yarns in shades of blue and white, sequins and bobbin type sewing needles. Pictures of rivers and streams showing fast and slow moving water.

Talk About

- The start of a river and how it might move e.g. trickling around pebbles etc. and how later on as it grows in size it might ripple, splash and swirl as it flows. Further on when it is a broad river it may appear as twists and eddies as it glides swiftly under bridges and past its banks on the way to the sea.
- Making a collection of words to describe the movement of water. Matching these words to the pictures of rivers and streams.
- Drawing and smudging chalk pastel colours together. Cutting pebble shapes out of coloured paper and sticking them on to a background.
- Sewing long and short stitches using yarn and a bobbin needle in an open weave fabric.

Doing

- Get a piece of grey sugar paper, either a rectangle or a circle, and some pieces of the coloured paper and foil. Cut pebble shapes of different sizes out of some of these papers and stick them on different parts of the background. Use a white chalk pastel to draw lines, with fairly large gaps between them, from one side of your paper to the other. Curve the lines around the pebble shapes as they pass and keep the lines running in the same direction. Allow some of them to meet and cross over. Choose further

chalk pastels that match the papers and use these colours to fill in the gaps between the lines. Work from the top of your paper downwards to avoid spoiling your work and try smudging and blending the colours together in some places.

- Get a strip of open weave fabric, a bobbin needle and some yarns. Choose the colour of yarn you want to use first, thread one end through the eye of your needle and tie a knot in the other end and begin sewing straight stitches of different lengths on to your fabric, making some of them go in different directions. When all your yarn has been used, choose a different colour and continue working in the same way until your fabric is filled. Add sequins to some of the stitches if you wish.

Display

Mount the stitching on grey paper leaving only a small margin around each one and display them as a block in the middle of the board. Spray the chalk drawings with hair spray before mounting them individually and displaying them in rows around the block. Print out the water words and use them as a border.

Waterfalls and Weirs

Equipment Needed
A long strip of transparent polythene or bubble wrap, scissors, glue, cellophane, foil, yarns, sequins, beads, tissue paper and other collage materials in shades of blue, white and turquoise. Pictures of waterfalls and weirs.

Talk About
*   What a waterfall is and what a weir is and the difference between them - one is man made and one is natural.
*   Famous waterfalls and where they are found in the world and the rivers they are on e.g. Niagara Falls, Victoria Falls etc.
*   How a waterfall or weir changes the movement of a river and the way it is used by boats etc.
*   The dangers of weirs and waterfalls and how rainfall alters and adds to both of them.
*   Cutting the various collage materials into small bits and sticking them on to a background.
*   How much glue to use and where to put it.
*   Working collaboratively on the background, sharing the decisions, the materials and the space.

Doing
*   Look at the long strip of transparent background material to see the area that has to be covered.
*   Look at the range of collage material to be used and discuss how it can be cut up, combined together and arranged. Consider that there will need to be several patches where the same materials are used and also that the materials can be combined together in different mixes and in different ways.
*   Decide how the work is going to be done e.g. in groups, with each child having an area to work on or as a class, with each child having a turn and choosing the area to work on.
*   The collage materials need to be selected by each individual, cut up if necessary and arranged and stuck on the transparent background. Some materials may look more interesting if they are folded or curled - such possibilities need to be explored before they are stuck down.
*   Patches of glue will need putting on the background and the different materials pressed firmly on to it.

Display
The work when dry will need to be draped from the top of a board onto the surface beneath where it could be lain over crumpled newspaper and boxes as the base of the waterfall. On either side of the created waterfall, pictures of waterfalls around the world found on the internet together with information about them plus poetry about waterfalls written by the children could be displayed.

Reflections

Equipment Needed

Pieces of black paper A4 size, grey sugar paper A4 size, scissors, glue and blue and white chalk pastels. Pictures showing reflections in water.

Talk About

- What a reflection is and surfaces around school in which they can see a reflection of themselves or reflections of other objects.
- How reflections show up better when the surface in which they are reflected is still- hence reflections in rivers, lakes and ponds are more striking when the surface of the water is like this.
- The reflections in the pictures and what they are of.
- Other images that they would expect to find reflected in the smooth running surface of a river. Make a list of these.
- Folding paper in half before drawing an image.
- Cutting the image out with the paper still folded to produce two identical images
- Drawing with chalk pastel.

Doing

- Get a piece of black paper and fold it in half. Keep the paper folded whilst drawing the outline of an image on it in white chalk. It needs to be an image similar to one of those in the pictures or from the list of other images seen as reflections.
- Whilst keeping the paper folded, cut the image out carefully and cut along the fold as well. You should end up with two images that are identical.
- Get a piece of grey sugar paper and fold in half in the same way that you folded your black paper i.e. either landscape or portrait.
- Open up the grey paper and in an upright position above the fold stick one of the images cut from black paper.
- Cut the second (identical) image into strips

taking care to keep the strips in order.
- Stick these strips in reverse order under the original image i.e. upside down with gaps between each strip as a reflected image.
- Carefully fill in the gaps between and around the images using blue and white pastel. Add a black line along the fold with a strip of paper if you wish.

Display

If all the children have worked with their paper folded the same way i.e. all portrait or all landscape then the individual pieces could be arranged so that each one touches its neighbour to create a long river bank with matching reflections. If the work is of different sizes, mount each one individually and display them in equally spaced rows around the original pictures of reflections.

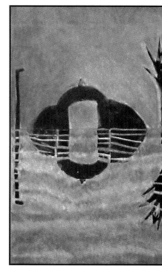

Finding Fish

Equipment Needed
Pieces of grey sugar paper A4 size, strips of black paper approx 10 cm wide, scissors, glue, drawing pencils, chalks or chalk pastels. Pictures of leisure activities involving water. Pictures of fresh water fish.

Talk About
- The pictures of leisure activities and what these activities are called.
- Which of these activities could take place on a river and which could not.
- Other leisure activities that can be enjoyed on or beside a river e.g. bird watching, walking etc.
- What your hobby if you are an angler.
- The names of different types of fresh water fish found in rivers, canals and ponds and what they look like - download these from the Internet.
- The equipment you need to go fishing and the fact that for many rivers or parts of rivers you need a licence before you can fish.
- Drawing different sorts of lines both with the edge of a chalk pastel and the side of a chalk pastel.
- Folding a strip of black paper in half several times, drawing an image on it and cutting this image out whilst the paper is still folded to reveal several identical images.

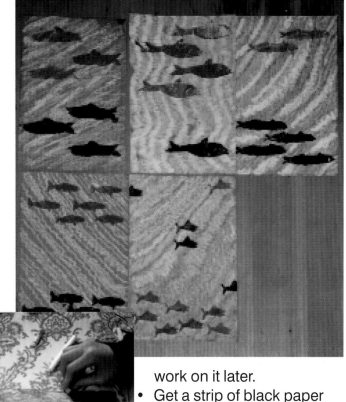

Doing
- Get a piece of grey sugar paper and some chalk pastels, choose those colours that you think match the colours seen in water.
- Use these colours to draw lines on your paper to represent the movement of water in a river e.g. wavy lines close together and further apart - some which are thick and some which are thin. Ensure this background is sprayed with hair spray by the teacher to prevent the work from smudging when you work on it later.
- Get a strip of black paper and fold it in half several times.
- Look at the different shapes in the pictures of fresh water fish and with a drawing pencil copy the outline shape of one of them on the top part of your folded strip. Cut this shape out carefully whilst the paper is still folded to get several identical images of your fish.
- Arrange your fish as a shoal all swimming in the same direction on part of your background paper and stick them down.

Display
Put a picture of a river in the middle of the display board - if possible find one that includes fishermen - surrounded by the pictures of different types of fresh water fish plus their names. Mount the chalk pictures individually and use them as a border to the display. Include written work from the children about the different sort of leisure activities that people use rivers for.

Changing Coastlines

Equipment Needed
Pieces of cream sugar paper A4 size and scrap pieces to practise on. Tissue paper, glue, paint, brushes, pieces of card to put it on, drawing pencils and thin strips of card to print with. Postcards that show beaches, cliffs and coastlines around the British Isles and travel brochures that show the same.

Talk About
*   The beaches in the pictures - the similarities and differences between them.
*   What the beaches are made up of - sand, shingle, mud flats, rocks, cliffs, sand dunes etc.
*   Where these beaches are on a map of the British Isles.
*   Tearing and crumpling tissue paper and sticking it on to a background - how much glue to use and where to put it.
*   Making different types of marks with a paintbrush by dabbing, swirling and dragging the brush as well as stroking and drawing with it on the paper.
*   Printing different sorts of marks with a piece of card dipped in paint.

Doing
*   You are going to make a picture of an imaginary beach using a mix of the different features seen on the beaches in the pictures.
*   Decide which features you are going to use and make a quick sketch on a piece of scrap paper.
*   Decide which part of your picture you are going to use tissue paper for, which part is going to be printed and which bit painted.
*   Get the colour of tissue paper you need and tear it and crumple it - for texture - before sticking it onto your background paper in the area you want it.
*   Put the colours of paint you need on a piece of card and with a brush begin adding these to your picture. Use different brushstrokes to

produce different textures in parts of your picture e.g. the texture of sand needs to appear different from rocks. Waves will be different again.

Experiment with different brushstrokes on your scrap paper before using them on your finished picture.
*   Use thin strips of card dipped in paint to print and add further detail to your picture e.g. straight and curved line, dots etc. Experiment with making these on scrap paper before adding them to your picture.

Display
Put the map of the British Isles in the middle of the board and surround it with the pictures of the different beaches - put each one in its appropriate place and attach it to the map with a piece of yarn. Mount the beach/ coastline pictures individually and display them in equally spaced rows around the central arrangement.

Colourful Cliffs

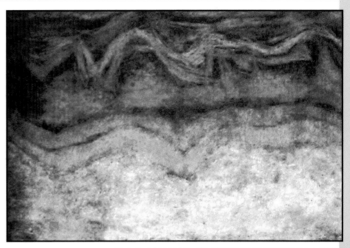

Equipment Needed
Paint, brushes, pieces of card to use as palettes, drawing pencils and scrap paper to practise on, chalk or chalk pastels, grey, black and white sugar paper A3 and A4 size. Pictures that show cliffs with patterns and distinct layers of coloured rocks in them.

Talk About
- The colours and patterns seen on the cliffs in the pictures.
- Why there are varieties of colours within some cliffs whereas others are similar all over.
- The names of different types of rocks that various cliffs are made up of e.g. granite, limestone, chalk etc.
- Where else different rock formations / cliffs can be seen - quarries, mountains, moors etc.
- Mixing the colours seen or finding similar colours in paint and chalk pastel.
- Drawing different lines and shapes with a brush and with chalk pastel.
- Working from the top of the paper downwards to avoid smudging either paint or chalk pastel.
- Drawing with the tip and the side of a chalk pastel.
- Choosing the size and colour of paper on which to work.

Doing
- Get a piece of paper the colour and size you want to work on, a piece of scrap paper and a drawing pencil.
- Look at the patterns on the rocks in the picture and decide the sort of patterns from them you are going to use in your work. Sketch them roughly on a scrap piece of paper.
- Now get the colours you are going to use in either paint or pastel. Mix other colours that you may need on your palette.

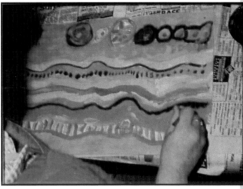

- Draw your pattern on your paper first with your finger, to get an idea of how big it will need to be and how often you can repeat the shapes in your pattern, before working with your chosen media.
- Work from the top of the paper downwards to avoid smudging and adding broad bands of colour first before drawing in any details.
- The chalk pastel drawings will need spraying with hair spray to fix them before they are mounted.

Display
Arrange the pictures of the different rock formations/cliffs in the middle of the board as a block. Mount the rock/cliff patterns individually and display them in equally spaced rows around the block of pictures. Print out the names of the different types of rocks and use these as a border around the edge of the display board.

Boats and Buildings

Equipment Needed

Paint, paintbrushes and pieces of card as a palette plus pieces of paper A3 size. Felt in assorted colours, net, scissors, glue (fabric glue if possible) sewing threads and needles. A large piece of plain fabric, if the final piece of work is to become a collaborative panel, or smaller pieces if it is to remain individual. Drawing pencils and scrap pieces of paper. Picture of boats in harbours, marinas, boatyards etc. plus buildings found along the coast - lighthouses, coastguard stations, lifeboat houses etc.

Talk About

- The different types of boats in the pictures - yachts, motor boats, fishing boats, liners etc. Who uses them and what they are used for - leisure, work etc.
- The different coastal buildings in the pictures, what their role is and why they are necessary. Finding any of these type of buildings on a map of the coast of the British Isles and discussing why they are in those particular places.
- Cutting felt and net into different shapes and gluing them on to a fabric background. Threading a needle, tying a knot in one end of the thread and sewing long and short straight stitches.
- Drawing outlines with a paintbrush before filling them in.

Doing

- Decide whether you are going to work on a building or a boat. If it is a building, look at the pictures for ideas, make a quick sketch and then get the paper and paint you need. Draw the main shapes in your picture first in a pale colour before filling them in and adding detail.
- If it is a boat, make a quick sketch of the type

of boat from the pictures. Get some pieces of coloured felt, scissors, glue and a background piece of fabric. Draw the shapes found on your boat on the felt with a

pencil before cutting them out and gluing them on the background. Get a needle and threads and using short and long straight stitches add detail to your boat e.g. the name, outlines of portholes etc.

- If it is to remain as an individual piece, add water and sky by cutting shapes out of net and sticking them down on the background. Overlay some of the pieces for interest. If it is to be part of a panel, cut round the outline of your boat and arrange it and glue it with the others on the background before adding sky, water and possibly buildings -together as a group.

Display

Arrange the textile panel on the board with a border of paper around it to make it appear mounted. Individual pieces could be mounted separately and displayed as a border around the pictures of boats. Mount the paintings of buildings individually and display them in rows with written work about each one underneath.

Horizons in View

Equipment Needed

Grey sugar paper 14 x 20 cm approx, black and white chalk pastels or white chalk and charcoal, pictures that show views from beaches/seafronts etc. looking towards the horizon.

Talk About

- That views when looking from the coast out to sea lead the eye from the land out across the sea and and into the distance. What the horizon is and where it can be seen in the pictures. The difference in size of objects that are seen close up and those that are seen in the distance. The detail that can be seen on objects that are close to and those that are seen in the distance and the size and detail that can be seen on objects in the area between the two.
- What foreground, middle ground and distance mean and which part of each pictures matches the foreground, middle ground and distance.
- Smudging black and white chalk pastels together to different shades of grey, black and white. Drawing with the edge of a chalk pastel.

Doing

- Look carefully at the seaside pictures that show views into the distance. You are going to draw an imaginary coastal view of your own looking into the distance (unless you have been on a trip to the sea-side and made a first hand sketch to work on.)
- Get a piece of grey paper and some black and white pastels. Put your paper landscape style and with the chalk pastels draw (with the pastels on their side) a wide band of white across and covering the top of the paper, a grey band across the centre by smudging a little black with the white and a dark grey band across the bottom of the paper by smudging more black with the white. These bands need to meet and merge

so that the whole paper is filled, however the three distinct bands of colour still need to be evident.

- These three bands are the foreground (the darkest band) the middle ground (the slightly paler band) and the distance (the palest band at the top).
- You now need to draw a line across the paper as the horizon - probably between the top and middle band. Above the horizon add a few clouds and in the middle ground the feint outline of waves, boats or a headland. In the darkest band you could draw in more detail other objects like rocks, grass, the railings of a promenade etc.
- Use the edge of a black chalk pastel for your drawing making it light and feint, in the distance, slightly darker in the middle ground and in the foreground the darkest and most detailed of all.

Display

Spray the drawings with hair spray before mounting them individually on black paper and displaying them in rows around a block of the sea side views originally looked at.

Pasted Peaks

Equipment Needed

Glue, scissors, white paper and black paper A4 size, oil pastel crayons, wax crayons and a collection of travel brochures. Pictures of mountains in different parts of the world.

Talk About

- The names of some of the different mountain ranges in the pictures and where they can be found on a map of the world e.g. Table Mountain, the Andes, the Alps etc.
- The shapes of the mountains and the type of vegetation or lack of vegetation on them - and why.
- The difference in appearance of some mountains at different times of the year e.g. the Alps are ski resorts in the winter and an attraction for walkers, climbers and tourists in the summer when they are free of snow.
- Where the mountains are in the British Isles and what they are called.
- Cutting out shapes from travel brochures and sticking them on to a background - how much glue to use and where to put it.
- Drawing spiky mountain shapes with oil pastels and wax crayons.
- Colouring in some of these shapes. Pressing on firmly for a rich covering of colour.
- Colours that will show up if a black background is chosen and those that won't.

Doing

- Choose either a piece of black or white paper and decide which way up you want to use it - either portrait or landscape style.
- Get a number of travel brochures and cut out a collection of mountains if possible from different parts of the world. Cut round the outline of these mountains leaving as little of the surrounding scenery as possible.
- Arrange these mountains on your background paper - beside, above, below, overlapping etc.
- When you are happy with your arrangement, stick it down.
- Use either or both the wax crayons and the oil pastels to draw lines around the mountains following their shapes - make the lines spiky where possible and leave gaps between them.
- Fill some of these gaps with colour - try to use the same colours seen on the mountains in the pictures.

Display

Put the pictures of the different mountains plus their names in the middle of the board or a map of the world with some of the mountain ranges marked. Mount the collages individually and arrange them in equally spaced rows around the map.

Rough Rocks

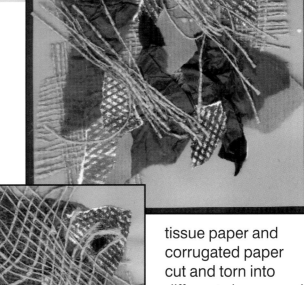

Equipment Needed

White paper of the newsprint variety, black and brown wax crayons, brown corrugated paper, brown and black tissue paper, scrim, brown and black sugar paper, scissors, glue and pieces of grey sugar paper A4 size. Pieces of rock that have a rough texture.

Talk About

- That a mountain environment is often a rough, rugged and rocky one.
- What the word 'texture' means. Words that describe different textures found in the room. Words that describe the textures found on the rocks themselves.
- The textures of the different materials to be used for the work.
- How to make a rubbing, by placing piece of paper over a textured surface and then crayoning across the paper to reveal a copy of the surface underneath.
- How to make tissue paper textured - by crumpling it before and as it is stuck down.
- How to make sugar paper appear textured - by tearing shapes out of it rather than cutting them.

Doing

- Get a piece of white paper and some brown and black crayons and make some rubbings of different surfaces in the classroom. Try taking rubbings from some of the collage materials as well e.g. scrim and corrugated paper and also the rocks that you looked at. Make some of the rubbings with one colour of crayon only and others with a combination of both. Move the paper into different positions on the same surface as you rub for added interest.
- Get a piece of grey paper and on it arrange some pieces of scrim, sugar paper, crumpled

tissue paper and corrugated paper cut and torn into different shapes and sizes. Leave gaps between some of them whilst allowing others to touch and overlap.
- Tear and cut the rubbings that you feel have been most successful and add them to fill the gaps in your collage.
- When you are happy with your arrangement stick it down carefully.
- You may need to make more rubbings or choose further collage materials to fill any gaps. Continue until the paper is full and your rough collage complete.

Display

Back the board with grey paper. Arrange the unmounted collages as a mountain shape in the middle of the board - some will need to be arranged at angles rather than straight and some may need to overlap. Cut some thin strips of black paper and use these to outline the shape of your mountain. Write or print with the computer 'texture words'. Cut them into strips and arrange them up one side of the mountain and down the other.

Multi-Coloured Mountains

Equipment Needed

Tissue paper, scissors, glue, grey sugar paper A3 and A4 size and pictures of mountains covered with different types of vegetation and showing different weather conditions or different times of the day.

Talk About

- The different mountains in the picture, the colours on them, the weather etc.
- How mountains appear in different colours when the light, the seasons and weather changes.
- Why weather at the top of the mountain and the vegetation that grows up there differs from that at the base and in the valleys below.
- How to tear tissue paper into strips.
- How to overlay tissue paper to create new colours.
- Cutting tissue paper into different shapes.
- Sticking tissue paper on to a background - how much glue to use and where to put it.
- Creating a landscape picture showing the shapes of mountains and the sky above them and area below them.

Doing

- Get a piece of A3 or A4 paper and decide which way you are going to work - with the paper either landscape or portrait style.
- Decide whether your picture is going to be of one mountain only or of a range of mountains.
- Get some tissue paper in the colours that match one of the pictures of mountains and tear them into strips of different lengths and thicknesses.
- Start with the sky and get the colours for this stuck down first - you may want to add

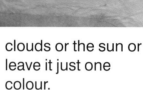

clouds or the sun or leave it just one colour.

- Next, arrange and then stick the strips down as you work to make the area below the mountain and the shape of the mountain itself.
- If you arrange the strips without sticking them down they are likely to blow away and get lost.
- Allow the strips to touch and overlap creating new colours along with the original ones.
- The top of your mountain/s should join or overlap the sky to complete your picture.

Display

Mount the pictures individually and arrange them in rows around the original pictures that form a block in the middle of the board. Write the names of the seasons and different types of weather conditions e.g. blizzards, fog, mist, appropriate to mountain environments and use them on strips as a border to the display.

Dressed for the Occasion

Equipment Needed

Thick brown card, scissors and glue, drawing pencils (4b-6b) a collection of hiking boots, walking shoes, oil pastel crayons and grey or cream sugar paper A4 and A3 size.

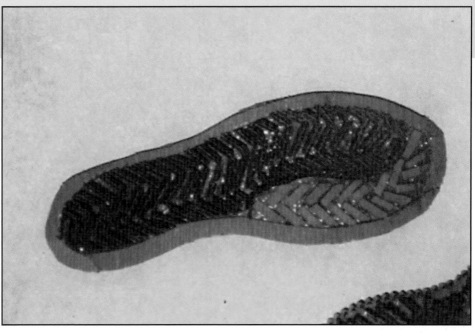

Talk About

- The fact that visiting and climbing mountains is an activity enjoyed by many people.
- The need to take care, use the proper equipment and wear the proper clothing when doing so - and why.
- The sort of things to take and wear to keep safe when walking in the mountains e.g. a whistle, a mobile phone, food, water, warm clothing, waterproof clothing, walking shoes or boots etc.
- How the weather can quickly change on a mountain and put people at risk if they are not properly prepared.
- How people are rescued if they get lost or have accidents in the mountains and who rescues them.
- The shapes and patterns on the soles of walking boots and shoes and how these help the soles to grip and why this is necessary.
- Cutting cardboard into small identical shapes. Sticking these shapes on to a background - how much glue to use and where to put it.
- Drawing with oil pastel crayons.

Doing

- Get a piece of brown card and a drawing pencil. Put one foot on the piece of card and draw round it. Cut the shape out carefully.
- Look at some of the different shapes on the soles of the hiking boots and walking shoes and draw some similar shapes on another piece of card and cut them out carefully.

- Arrange them to form a pattern or groups of patterns on the foot/ shoe sole you cut out and stick them down carefully.
- Make an observational drawing of a pair of walking shoes or boots. Arrange the boots/shoes in a group e.g. one upright one on its side and look at the arrangement carefully.
- Get a piece of paper either A3 or A4 depending on how big you want to make your drawing and sketch the outline shapes of the shoes/boots with a pencil.
- Add colour and detail to your drawing using the oil pastel crayons matching the colours as carefully as you can.

Display

Arrange the shoe soles in a group as though they are walking across the board. Mount the drawings and use them as a border along the top and bottom of the board.

Foreign Flowers

Equipment Needed

Paint, paintbrushes, pieces of card to put it on, some unusual and interesting flowers from warmer countries e.g. Heliconias, Anthuriums etc. (from a Florist), pictures of exotic flowers, pieces of white paper A3 size.

Talk About

- Where St Lucia is on the world map and the sort of climate it has and how the climate there is different from here - and why.
- Because of the different climate, the plants and flowers that grow in St Lucia will be different from those that grow in this country.
- Many of the indoor house plants at garden centres and in our homes are native to and grow wild in warmer countries.
- The colours and shapes of the flowers in the pictures - those they like best and why.
- Drawing flower head shapes with a paintbrush.
- Mixing bright colours of paint.
- Making paint lighter. Using a lot of white and a little colour.

Doing

- You are going to paint a collection of imaginary flower heads using actual flower heads as a stimulus for ideas.
- Get a paintbrush and a piece of paper and with a pale shade of paint, draw the outline of several different sized flower heads.
- Mix some bright colours of paint to fill in these shapes.
- Fill in the background around the flowers with different shades of green - there is lots of tropical greenery in St Lucia.
- Finally use your paintbrush to draw and add detail to your work.
- As well as individual work, large scale collaborative flowerheads could be made. The children will need to work in groups and each group needs to use only one colour of

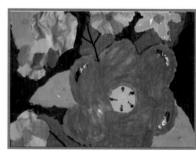

paint plus white.
- Each child cuts a petal shape out of white paper and fills it with matching bands of colour. A band of pure colour is painted in the middle of each petal followed either side by a paler band. More bands are added, each one slightly paler than the one before until both edges of the petals are reached.
- The petals are then attached to a central coloured circle to become a large exotic flowerhead.

Display

Arrange the paintings as a block so that they touch each other to make a tropical flower garden. Arrange the large flower heads down the sides of the display to frame it. Put pictures of tropical flowers, and house plants that come from the tropics on a surface under the display.

Beautiful Birds

Equipment Needed

Newspaper, masking tape, paper plates, coloured feathers, glue, tissue paper, thin strips of coloured paper and card, oil pastel crayons plus pieces of grey sugar paper A4 size. Pictures of the types of birds found in tropical rainforests.

Talk About

- The vegetation covered mountains, glossy rainforests and banana plantations on St Lucia that would be home for many different types of birds.
- Birds that are familiar to them in this country and the difference between them and the birds in the pictures.
- Making parcels out of newspaper and taping the parcels together with masking tape.
- Tearing tissue paper into small pieces.
- Folding and curling thin strips of paper and card.
- Drawing with oil pastels.

Doing

- Make a new type of tropical bird to live on St Lucia using the pictures of birds as a stimulus for ideas.
- Get some newspaper, scrunch it and wrap it in other layers to make a parcel for the body of your bird. Tape the parcel together with masking tape so that it doesn't open up. Make a smaller parcel for the head and tape it on to the body.
- Cut a paper plate in half and stick each half on top of the body, either side of the head, as wings, and tape on some coloured feathers as a tail.
- Choose the colours of tissue paper you want to use, tear them into small pieces and glue them on to cover the wings, head and body.

Allow them to touch and overlap. You may need more than one layer to hide the construction underneath.

- Curl and fold some of the coloured strips of paper and card and use them to further decorate the tail and add plumage to the head.
- Print the eyes with a cotton bud dipped in paint and make the beak out of a folded strip of card cut to a point.
- Once your bird is complete and dry, get a piece of sugar paper and some oil pastel crayons and make an observational drawing of it. Start with the outline before adding colour and detail.
- Draw leaves of different sizes and shapes in various shades of green to create a background around your bird as though it is in a tropical rainforest.

Display

Put all the unmounted oil pastel drawings together as a block in the middle of the board, with a narrow border of another colour round them so that they appear mounted. Arrange the 3D birds on green leaves cut from different shades of paper on a surface underneath the board.

Under the Sea

Equipment Needed

Marbling inks, a shallow tray, white paper in a size that matches the size of the top of the tray, coloured paper, paint, brushes, small paper plates, glue and pictures of coral reefs and fish found around them in tropical waters.

Talk About

- That St Lucia is an island sheltered by coral reefs. What a reef is and what coral is.
- What equipment you need to swim under water and visit a coral reef.
- The sort of fish and plants that live on and around a reef in tropical waters - the colours, sizes and shapes of the fish in the pictures.
- That the tropical fish kept in tanks in this country are native to seas in the tropics.
- How to use marbling inks (See Step by Step Art 3 page 31).
- Tearing coloured paper into strips and shapes and sticking them on to a background - how much glue to use and where to put it.

Doing

- Look at the colours of the water in the pictures of the sea around St Lucia and choose the colours of marbling inks that match those colours.
- Put a few drops of each of these colours into the water in a shallow tray, swirl them around to break them up before laying a piece of paper on to the water and tapping it so that the whole of the surface touches the paper.
- Lift the paper off to reveal the print. Take a second print from the same tray without adding any more ink - this print will be different from the first and probably paler.
- When the marbling prints are dry decide which one you want to use for your underwater picture.
- Get some coloured paper and tear it into shapes of different sizes for fish, perhaps

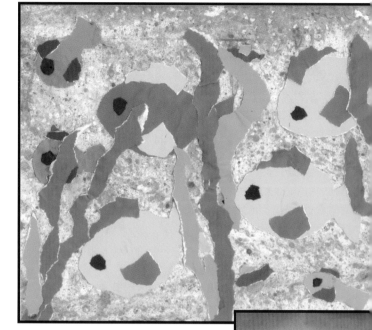

using different colours for their fins and tails.
- Arrange these fish, in groups, on your marbled background. When you are happy with your arrangement stick it down.
- Now tear some strips and some shapes with holes in them as the plant life and coral found on a reef.
- Get a small paper plate and tear and stick shapes on it to become the tail and the fins before tearing smaller shapes as scales to cover the plate.
- Colour the area around the eye with paint and print the eye itself with a finger dipped in paint. Cut a slit for the mouth and outline it with paint.

Display

Arrange the marbled pictures unmounted as a block to make a large underwater scene in the middle of the board. Use the paper plate fish as a border around the edge of the block.

Caribbean Colours

Equipment Needed

White oil pastel crayons, white wax crayons, white paper and coloured paper A4 size, paint, paintbrushes, pieces of card to put it on and thin strips of card. Pictures of the landscape and coast of St Lucia. Examples of batik and brightly, coloured, patterned fabric.

Talk About

- The shops and stalls in St Lucia having plenty of examples of local crafts for sale to visitors and tourists. These include, woodcarving, basket making, screen printing and batik.
- How batik is done - drawing on fabric with hot wax then dipping the fabric into different coloured dyes, adding more drawing and finally cracking and removing the wax. The wax prevents the colour penetrating the fabric and creates the outline of shapes and areas of different colours in a design.
- The bright colours and patterns on the fabrics.
- The landscape pictures of St Lucia and the shapes and colours in them that could be used in a pattern e.g. palm trees, sunsets etc.
- Naming and describing the colours.
- Drawing with white wax crayons or white oil pastel on white paper and coloured paper and adding bands of paint over the drawing.
- Printing different sorts of lines with the edge of a strip of card dipped in paint.

Doing

- Get a piece of white paper and either a white wax crayon or a white oil pastel.
- Decide the shapes (from the landscape of St Lucia) that you are going to use in your pattern and draw them several times on your piece of white paper.
- Now choose a bright colour of paint, dip a brush in water then paint and drag it across your pattern to reveal the shapes you have drawn.

- You could use the same colour all over your pattern or several bands of different bright colour. Use the colours seen in the pictures of St Lucia.
- Add further detail to your pattern by adding different lines around, under and between the shapes using a strip of card dipped in paint.
- Make a further, different, wax resist pattern this time using a coloured paper as a background.
- As well as individual wax resist patterns the children could work collaboratively on a large scale one.

Display

Mount the individual pieces of work and arrange them with very narrow gaps between them in the middle of a board surrounded by pictures of the landscape of St Lucia. Arrange the bright coloured pieces of fabric under the display. Put the large scale piece of work in the middle of the board surrounded with landscape pictures as described previously.

Lots of Litter

Equipment Needed

Paint, paintbrushes and pieces of card to use as palettes, white paper in assorted sizes, felt tip pens, drawing pencils (4b-6b) wax crayons and examples of different paper packaging e.g. empty crisp packets that make up a lot of the litter found in the environment.

Talk About

- What litter is and where it is often seen in the locality.
- Where litter should be disposed of and where litter bins are sighted in the locality - and why they are placed there e.g. outside shops.
- How the roads and pavements are cleaned and made litter free and how and when household rubbish is collected and where it is taken.
- Notices in public places to warn us about dropping litter/making a mess and the fines that will have to be paid if we are caught breaking these rules.
- What goes on a poster or sign to attract people's attention - the message/ image needs to be simple and striking.
- Ideas for improving the environment and preventing 'litter louts".
- The colours and shapes of the packaging to be drawn or painted and the position of the lettering on it.
- Drawing with felt tip pens, paintbrushes and wax crayons.

Doing

- If you are going to make a poster choose a piece of paper A4 size or slightly larger. Place it portrait or landscape way up, decide what you are going to draw and what you are going to write and how these are going to be arranged on your poster. Make sure the message is clear. Sketch your design lightly at first before filling it in with paint and adding outlines using felt tip pens.

- If you are going to make an observational drawing or painting of one piece or several pieces of rubbish, select the rubbish, choose a piece of white paper of a size you think is appropriate and the colours of paint or wax crayons that match it. If it is going to be padded and become part of a 3D display it will need to be drawn on a piece of paper that is larger than the actual rubbish.

- Draw or paint the outline shape of your piece of rubbish and the lettering on it first in a pale colour before filling it in and finally outlining the letter shapes.

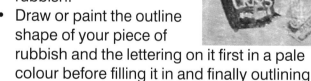

Display

There are several ways this work could be displayed. The drawings of groups of rubbish could be individually mounted and displayed in equally spaced rows. The drawings of individual pieces of rubbish could be cut out and become a collaborative picture of an overlapping collection of rubbish. The large scale paintings could be cut out, padded at the back wth crumpled newspaper as they are attached to the board. Fasten further crumpled pieces of news paper between the work for greater effect.

Ready to Recycle

Equipment Needed
Masking tape, scissors, glue, paint, brushes, pieces of card to put the paint on, magazines, newspapers, plastic bottles, empty drinks cans and pieces of brown cardboard. Small pieces of black and white paper plus pictures of dinosaurs.

Talk About
• What recycling means. The different bins and boxes that are now provided to houses for the collection of different categories of rubbish - what these categories are and who collects the rubbish.
• Where the local recycling banks are - often in car parks in town centres or near large stores - and what can be taken there for recycling.
• Tearing and cutting masking tape into strips.
• Taping different solid shapes together with masking tape.
• Making newspaper parcels of different sizes and fastening them together with masking tape.
• Taping newspaper parcels on to the solid shapes.
• Cutting black and white paper into circular shapes, triangles and strips.
• The shapes of the heads, bodies, legs etc. of the dinosaurs in the pictures.
• Making a new dinosaur - A Recyclasaurus - from the range of reclaimed materials.

Doing
• Look at the range of reclaimed materials carefully before selecting those from which to make a model.
• Try standing the shapes next to each other, balancing on top of each other etc. to see how they fit together before using the tape to fasten them together. Decide whether you need to make any newspaper parcels to add to or pad out your model to improve its shape.

• Fasten these to your model with tape as well.
• Use paint to colour and disguise the masking tape by painting it to match the different materials it is fastened to.
• Leave most of the recycled materials on show perhaps adding a pattern to part of your model e.g. the head or body using magazines.
• Cut eyes out of the black and white paper and add them to the head of your Recyclasaurus. Add spiky spines or a tail, horns or claws using the black paper if you wish.

Display
Arrange the models on individual squares of black paper on a flat surface under a board or on shelves made from boxes attached to the board (See Step by Step Display in the Primary School page 28). Add written work about recycling and photographs of the children making their models together with descriptions as to how they were made to the board.

Pollution and Noise

Equipment Needed

Marbling ink, a shallow tray, white and grey paper that will fit in the tray, white paint, pieces of card to put it on, strips of card and reclaimed materials to print with, black paper A3 size, a computer and a printer. Pictures of pollution and agents of pollution - smoking chimneys, car exhausts, mobile phone masts, pylons etc.

Talk About

- What pollution is and the damage it can do to the environment.
- The parts of the environment that can be damaged by pollution that can affect us all.
- Ways and means that are being used to try and reduce pollution.
- Noises we hear that irritate and annoy us - in school, at home, in the street etc. and words that describe them.
- Colours we associate with things that are sad, bad, dangerous, destructive or frightening and why.
- How to use marbling inks to make a print (see Step by Step Art 3 page 31).
- Printing with reclaimed materials dipped in white paint on black paper.
- Using different fonts in large sizes to write and print noise words using a computer.

Doing

- Choose the colours of marbling ink that you associate with pollution and put a few drops of each in the marbling tray partly filled with water.
- Lay a piece of grey or white paper on the surface of the water, tap it gently so that it all sits on the water and take a print. Lift the paper off and allow it to dry.
- Get a black piece of paper, some white paint and some strips of card and reclaimed materials. Look carefully at the pictures that show some of the sources of pollution and decide which ones you are going to include

in your picture.

- Use a strip of card dipped in paint to print the outline of the main shapes to start with before filling them in and adding to them using other reclaimed materials dipped in paint.

- Make a list of 'noise' words - as many as you can.
- Use the computer and a range of different fonts in large sizes to write (in black) and

print out your 'noise' words e.g. bang, zoom, thump, whistle etc. Try and use a different font for each one.

Display

Mount the prints individually on grey paper. Back the board in black and arrange the prints in rows with large gaps between some of them. Fill these gaps with puddle shapes cut from the pieces of marbling. Add the printed noise words as a border around the display and in some of the gaps.

On the Trail of Traffic

Equipment Needed

Paint brushes, paint and pieces of card to put it on, white paper A4 size, drawing pencils (4b-6b), grey sugar paper A3 size, glue, an assortment of different coloured papers, a copy of the Highway Code and a collection of model cars, buses, lorries etc.

Talk About

*   The sort of traffic they see on the way to school, the traffic that passes the school and the traffic that visits the school. The time of day when the traffic is busiest and why. The time of day when it is quietest and why.
*   Signs in the locality and in the Highway Code that restrict the speed of traffic or isolate and separate traffic e.g. cycle tracks and bus lanes.
*   Looking carefully at the shapes of the model cars, lorries etc. the different parts of them and how they fit together.
*   Making an observational drawing of a car, bus lorry etc. using a paintbrush.
*   Making an observational drawing of a car, bus, lorry etc. in collage using torn pieces of paper.
*   Drawing in paint, traffic calming signs from pictures of signs in the locality and in the Highway Code.

Doing

*   If you are going to paint a picture of a car, bus etc. get a piece of grey A3 paper and the model vehicle that you are going to copy. As you are going to paint it larger than the actual model, draw it on the paper with your finger first, to get an idea of the size it will need to be before drawing its outline with a pale shade of paint (e.g. grey) and then filling it in.
*   If you are going to make a collage of a car,

bus etc. get a piece of A4 paper, some glue, the model vehicle that you are going to copy and the different colours of paper that match it. Sketch the outline of the vehicle lightly with a pencil before tearing the coloured paper into different shaped pieces and arranging them to fill it in before gluing them down.

*   If you are going to make a traffic calming painting, get a piece of grey sugar paper and on it draw the outlines in a pale shade of paint of some of the traffic calming signs seen in the pictures and in the Highway Code. Draw them fairly large and at different angles on the paper. The same sign can be repeated more than once. Fill them in once you have finished drawing and decide how you are going to fill the gaps between the signs - you could add road markings, tyre tracks or wheel shapes etc.

Display

The traffic calming paintings could be displayed as a block surrounded by the individually mounted collages. The painted vehicles could be cut out and displayed both behind and next to each other as in a traffic jam.

Danger and Destruction

Equipment Needed

Pieces of white paper A3 and A4 size, paint, brushes, pieces of card to put it on, felt tip pens, drawing pencils (4b-6b), oil pastel crayons, glue, a computer and a printer, pictures of rainforests, polar ice caps, coral reefs etc. and endangered species.

Talk About

- The parts of the world shown in the pictures and where they are on the globe. Why these areas are under threat and what is threatening them.
- The names of endangered species, where they are found and why they are under threat.
- What effects these changes to the environment are having and will have in the future unless they are stopped.
- Species of birds, insects, animals and plants that are under threat in this country and why.
- Posters and road signs that warn of different types of danger. Designing a poster highlighting a part of the world under threat or designing a road sign for a species under threat. Including a written message on the poster or road sign using self drawn lettering or writing it on the computer and cutting it out. How the images and the written message should be arranged together. Working with the different types of media - individually and collaboratively.

Doing

- Decide whether you are going to design a poster or a road sign. For a poster you will need A3 paper and for a road sign A4.
- Get the pictures you need as a stimulus either of an endangered species (for a road sign) or a place on the planet under threat (plus some of the species that live there if you want) for a poster.
- Decide what you are going to include in your design and sketch the outline of the main

shapes lightly with a pencil. Remember to leave space for the lettering. Choose the media you want to use to add colour and detail to your design - you could use one media e.g. paint on its own or a combination for different parts of your work. Oil pastel drawing on top of painting works particularly well.

- Once your design is coloured either add the letters for the message on it, colour them in and then outline them or write them on the computer, print them, cut them out and add them to your design.

Display

Mount the posters individually and display them in rows around a picture of the globe (arrows to the areas under threat). Cut out the road signs and display them on a black background around a block of pictures and written work about endangered species.

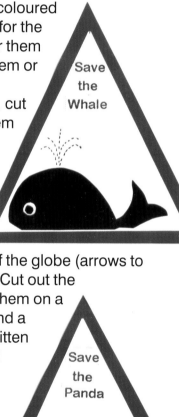